Safety First

English for Health and Safety

John Chrimes

Resource Book

Published by
Garnet Publishing Ltd.
8 Southern Court
South Street
Reading RG1 4QS, UK

www.garneteducation.com

ISBN: 978 1 85964 553 6

British Library Cataloguing-in-Publication Data
A catalogue record for this book is available from the British Library.

Acknowledgement
Special thanks to the project consultants, Fiona McGarry and Chris Gough, for their work in
shaping the tasks.

Production
Project manager: Kate Kemp
Project consultants: Chris Gough, Fiona McGarry, Rod Webb
Editorial: Fiona Dempsey, Kate Kemp, Karen Kinnair-Pugh
Design and layout: Christin Helen Auth, Mike Hinks
Illustration: Calvin Innes, Doug Nash
Photography: K. Stenlake, Bob House, istockphoto.com
Audio: Recorded at Motivation Sound Studios, produced by EFS Television
                      Production Ltd.

Printed and bound in Lebanon by International Press: interpress@int-press.com

Contents

Book map

Unit	Title	Topics/Vocabulary	Language/Functions	Activities
1	Basics of health and safety	General health and safety terms Different health and safety topics Numbers and units of measurement	Naming and spelling objects and places connected with health and safety Asking for and giving personal information	Form-filling Listening to an overview of the course and completing a course outline mind map Reading and making decisions to complete a health and safety maze Role play: greetings and introductions
2	Hazards and risk assessment	Hazard types Hazard prevention and control measures Language of graphs and trends	Identifying and describing site hazards and evaluating risks Giving opinions and making decisions Describing trends and using statistics	Listening to a lecture on risk assessment stages Filling in a risk assessment form Role play: a decision-making meeting Role play: social conversations
3	Personal Protective Equipment (PPE)	Parts of the body and types of PPE Position and location vocabulary Workplace organization	Talking about appropriate PPE use and misuse Describing where things are Asking and answering questions about company structure and workplace organization	Reading and making decisions to complete a PPE dilemma maze Writing e-mails using appropriate formal/informal style Filling in a table and drawing an organizational diagram Role play: giving directions and talking about the weather
4	Hand-held safety equipment	Hand tools and associated hazards Power tools and associated hazards Shape vocabulary	Describing tools, their uses and potential hazards Asking and answering questions as part of a tool inspection Discussing permit to work procedure	Listening to a lecture on equipment safety Reading and following safety instructions for using a chainsaw Identifying and completing a permit to work form Role play: discussing future plans
5	Mechanical equipment	Mechanical equipment parts, hazards and control measures Different types of safety signs Gauges and measuring devices	Using the imperative to explain mechanical hazard preventions and warnings Describing changes in pressure and quantity Discussing excavation site safety	Listening to a lecture on mechanical equipment safety Describing safety signs in detail Identifying/defining hazards and discussing problems in pictures Role play: describing faults and malfunctions and offering solutions
6	Transport safety	Transport vocabulary, including vehicles and road signs Verbs of movement and injury, e.g., *fall, trip, slip* Places/departments in a company	Discussing and giving details of transport hazards, accidents and prevention measures Asking for and giving directions using a workplace map Practising language for rules and regulations in the context of transport	Listening to a lecture on transport safety for pedestrians Writing e-mails giving details of accidents Reading and making decisions to complete a forklift safety maze Role play: giving information about recent events
7	Working at height	Height equipment and PPE Hazards associated with working at height Adjectives and nouns to describe dimensions and units of quantity	Describing rules and signs connected with ladder safety Discussing hazards and PPE connected with working at height Asking and answering questions about dimensions and quantity	Listening to a lecture about ladder safety Reading and responding to different types of written correspondence Correcting and editing written work Role play: starting conversations

Unit	Title	Topics/Vocabulary	Language/Functions	Activities
8	Workplace manual handling	Vehicles and equipment used for handling loads Verbs, adjectives and adverbs associated with handling and handling hazards Types of containers	Following and giving instructions Discussing and describing types of containers Negotiating prices and conditions of goods deliveries	Listening to a lecture on manual handling statistics and procedures Reading instructions from a manual and labeling a diagram Transferring information from notes to risk assessment forms Role play: making requests and suggestions
9	Fire safety	Fire safety procedures and equipment Fire hazards and signs Ordinal numbers and dates	Asking about and describing fire signs Identifying and explaining fire hazards Asking and answering questions about fire procedures	Listening to a lecture on fire safety and extinguisher types Reading short news items about different types of fires Exchanging information and completing a text Role play: looking at pros and cons of a situation
10	Chemical safety and hazardous substances	Types of hazardous chemicals Chemical hazard prevention Safety labels and substance identification	Hypothesising and making deductions in order to identify hazards and solve problems Explaining information on hazardous substance labels Giving safety advice about hazardous substances using the imperative	Listening to a lecture on hazardous chemicals Reading problem-solving texts about hazardous chemicals Reading and writing safety labels Role play: asking for and giving advice
11	Electrical safety	Electrical hazards Electrical injuries and first aid Adjectives and comparative adjectives to describe workplace items	Asking about and explaining electrical hazards and equipment Comparing items, places and people in the workplace Asking for and exchanging information in order to solve a problem	Listening to a lecture about electrical safety Reading and completing electrical safety posters Reading and making decisions to complete an electric shock dilemma maze Role play: discussing cause and effect
12	First aid and injury	Body parts, injuries and treatments First-aid items Verbs and adjectives to describe damage to tools and equipment	Asking and answering questions about health problems and their treatment Discussing first-aid items that are needed for different situations Describing different types of damage to equipment and tools	Discussing injuries and completing a table with notes on cause and treatment Writing and spelling body parts, injuries, damage and treatments via wordsearches and puzzles Listening to a lecture on the ABC of first aid Role play: explaining procedures and processes
13	Incident reports	Accident/emergency vocabulary Terms connected with incident report forms	Discussing accidents and speculating about what happened Asking for and giving details of incidents and accidents Ordering events in a narrative sequence	Listening to a lecture on incident reports and becoming familiar with sections of incident report forms Writing and amending incident report forms Reading texts describing accidents and sequencing events Role play: giving detailed descriptions
14	Other hazards	Injuries and terms connected with noise, vibration and ergonomics Superlative adjectives to describe workers Safety inspection topics/review of hazard vocabulary	Using superlatives to compare things and personnel Describing noise, vibration and ergonomic issues using appropriate terms and acronyms Making recommendations for improving safety procedures	Listening to a lecture that recaps on and introduces new types of hazards Reading case studies and making recommendations Reading a safety inspection report Role play: checking information

Introduction

Aims

Safety First is an ESP course providing language and communication support for health and safety topics in technical, industrial and workplace situations. The course follows health and safety themes and provides practical contexts for high-frequency lexis connected with the workplace. It also builds essential workplace language skills, such as following instructions and form-filling. Each unit contains imaginative and challenging tasks to stimulate communication through problem-solving. Students become familiar with typical health and safety scenarios by following Jimmy, a trainee at ZemTeQ, through his day-to-day health and safety training.

Structure

The book is divided into topic-based units, including: Workplace manual handling, Working at height, Fire safety, Electrical safety, First aid and injury, and Incident reports. Units contain:

- an audio recording of a health and safety training seminar
- work-based conversation/small talk listening and practice
- problem-solving activities using key vocabulary
- practice activities for vocabulary, to aid transfer
- authentic texts, including forms and signs

Working with the course

As a resource book: *Safety First* can be used as a stand-alone resource for students and teachers to follow as a core text. The theme-based approach mirrors the way health and safety is taught in the workplace. The course provides core vocabulary for each theme and allows students to practise speaking, listening, reading and writing skills in contexts connected with the topic. As students work collaboratively to solve specific problems, they are encouraged to activate the language from the unit.

As supplementary material: *Safety First* can also be used as a supplementary resource on other courses that require health and safety input. In particular, it would be suitable for students on technical English courses or work-based ESP courses where only certain aspects of health and safety need be covered.

Teacher's Book: Step-by-step teaching notes are supplied for each lesson. These are for guidance only, as each lesson will depend on the students and their particular circumstances. Lesson notes come with full answers and transcripts of the listening.

Basics of health and safety

1 What do you know?: Health and safety

Objective: To focus on key health and safety vocabulary and practise talking about basic concepts.

▶ 1 Find the words

Try to find 14 words connected to health and safety in the wordsearch.

K	P	Q	P	K	J	X	L	G	E	D	C	G	I	O
H	E	J	T	A	Y	B	I	R	Q	J	W	P	A	O
A	R	E	I	K	W	Q	U	W	B	M	A	S	M	L
N	M	L	Y	V	V	J	A	I	L	R	R	I	E	M
D	I	I	T	N	N	L	H	G	E	E	X	G	O	T
T	T	F	O	I	M	B	G	D	M	I	K	N	C	L
O	W	F	X	D	P	K	D	M	U	L	C	E	O	S
O	L	E	I	N	A	A	A	N	T	A	T	G	R	L
L	N	C	C	K	L	H	Y	W	Y	O	J	D	E	A
W	V	S	N	C	O	N	S	T	R	U	C	T	P	G
M	H	L	M	A	U	I	I	P	S	W	P	O	O	Q
V	X	X	O	N	F	I	R	E	E	X	I	T	R	O
P	V	G	H	A	Z	A	R	D	Y	Y	K	J	T	S
P	J	X	X	Y	P	B	R	E	A	T	H	I	N	G
Q	W	R	O	B	G	A	O	R	R	I	S	K	A	P

▶ 2 Walk and talk

a Discuss the questions below with a partner and answer as many as you can.

1. What type of accident kills most construction workers?
2. What does a risk assessment do?
3. How should you stand to lift a load from the floor?
4. Why shouldn't you paint a ladder?
5. What should you do if your PPE is damaged?
6. How often should you inspect hand tools like hammers?
7. What should you do if you hear the fire alarm?
8. What colour are fire exit signs?
9. When is a site vehicle likely to injure a pedestrian?
10. What are two recommended ways to protect your hearing?
11. What two things must you do when you use an extension cable?
12. What should you do if you think a co-worker has a broken leg?

b Walk around the class, asking and answering the questions with as many people as possible.

▶ 3 What do you think?

a Complete the sentences below with your ideas and compare your answers with a partner.

1. Accidents happen because ...
2. First aid can ...
3. Electricity is dangerous when ...
4. Ladders are not hazardous if ...
5. The PPE I need is ...
6. The best thing about my job is ...
7. The difficult part of my job is ...
8. My worst accident was ...
9. The best part of training is ...
10. English is important for my job because ...

b Share your ideas with the class.

Alphabet A–Z

Objectives: To practise naming and spelling objects and places connected with health and safety. To pronounce English letters correctly.

▶ 1 Point and say

Work in groups. Take it in turns to point to the letters and say them correctly. See who can name all the letters in the shortest time.

▶ 2 Name the items

Each item below starts with a different letter of the alphabet. Work in groups to write a list of the items in alphabetical order. See which group can finish first.

▶ 3 Speak, listen and write

In partners, practise spelling out some of the key words and expressions from this lesson.

a Student A should dictate the letters of five words, without pausing between words.

b Student B should write down the letters and then decide where each word begins and ends.

c Swap roles.

3 | Personal information

Objectives: To practise asking for and giving personal information and filling in forms.

▶ **1** ⦿ **1:1 Listen and write**

You are going to listen to health and safety lectures throughout this course. Your lecturer is Richard. Listen to Richard introduce himself and fill in his Employee Information Card (EIC).

ZemTeQ Employee Information Card

Please fill out this information card. It will provide much needed data for our Human Resources Dept.

Name: _____ _____ _____   **Employee #:** _____
Last Name   First Name   Title

Current Address:
Street _____ City _____ Zip _____ Phone (day) _____

                                                                                    Phone (night) _____

Previous Address:
Street _____ City _____ Zip _____

How long at current address? _____   **How long at previous address?** _____

In the event of an emergency, please notify:

1 _____   2 _____
Name   Name

_____   _____
Address   Address

_____   _____
Relationship   Relationship

_____   _____
Phone (day)   (night)   Phone (day)   (night)

Personal Information:

Date of birth: _____/_____/_____   Gender: ☐ Male   ☐ Female

Have you been employed here before? ☐ Yes   ☐ No   If yes, please tell us when: _____/_____/_____

Do you have any special certifications or clearances? _____
_____
_____

Voluntary Personal Information:
_____
_____
_____
_____

▶ **2 Ask and write**

Read the prompts on page 135 and write the full questions. Then talk to a partner and write down their answers.

▶ **3 Tell the class**

Tell the class about the student you talked to. The class can then ask him/her more detailed questions.

Objectives: To practise listening to descriptions of course components. To practise organizing course-related vocabulary into groups using a mind map.

▶ **1** ⊚ **1:2 Listen and write**

Listen to Richard give an outline of a health and safety course.

a Write down the 14 main topics he will cover.

1 _General workplace health and safety_ n
2 _____ ____
3 _____ ____
4 _____ ____
5 _____ ____
6 _____ ____
7 _____ ____
8 _____ ____
9 _____ ____
10 _____ ____
11 _____ ____
12 _____ ____
13 _____ ____
14 _____ ____

b Match the pictures (a–n) from the lecture to the 14 subjects.

a

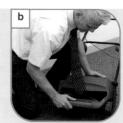
b

c

d

e

f

g

h

i

j

k

l

m

n

▶ **2** **Identify**

Which health and safety subjects/items do these signs represent?

1

2

3

4

5

6

7

8

9

10

11

12

13

14

15

▶ 3   Complete a mind map

Below is a mind map that a student drew in one of the health and safety lectures last year. The subject is PPE, one of the 14 topics mentioned in Task 1. Can you complete the labels?

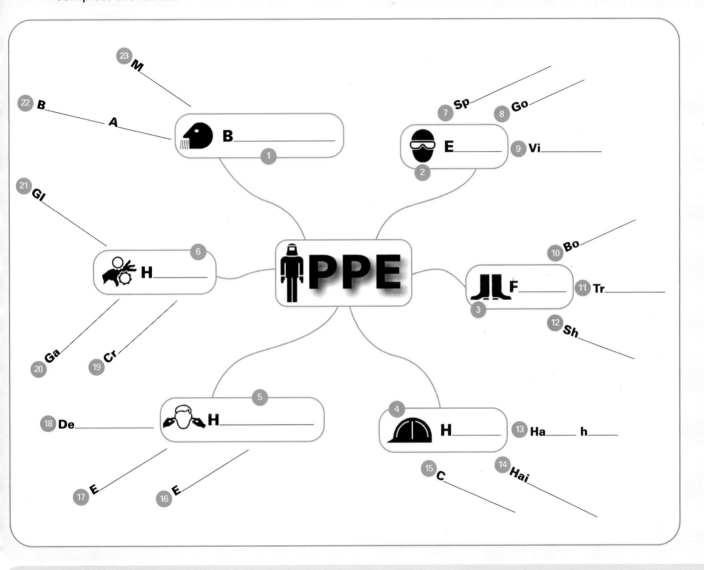

▶ 4   Draw a mind map

a With a partner, choose one of the subjects from Task 1 and draw a mind map to show any information you know about the subject. Try to include important equipment and rules or signs.

b When you have finished, put the mind maps on the wall around the class.

c Walk around and look at each map as though you were in a gallery. Discuss any new words and ideas. Make a list of new terms.

Objective: To practise careful reading and listening in order to make decisions.

▶ **1** **Match and ask**

a Match the verbs (a–f) with the questions (1–6).

1 How do you ___ spills at home?

2 Do you ___ prices before you buy things?

3 If you are angry, what do you do to ___?

4 Do you ___ working if you have a headache?

5 Did you ___ shelves at home?

6 Do you ___ to see your friends at the weekend?

a drop in   **b** check out
c carry on   **d** put up
e clean up   **f** calm down

b With a partner, ask and answer the questions.

▶ **2** **Read, listen and decide**

Work in groups of three. Take it in turns to read out the situation in each step and decide which way to go. Find your way out of the maze by answering correctly.

1 You work in ZemTeQ's Workshop 3. You are a good worker and not normally late. However, your child was sick last week and you were late three times. Your shift manager warned: 'Don't be late again or I'll have to take action'. Coming to work, you saw an accident and stopped to help. You arrive late and worried. **Go to 6**

2 You get bored with looking and start work. **Go to 5**

3 You meet the shift manager in the corridor. You make an excuse for being late and continue. **Go to 16**

4 You chat for a long time. He reminds you it is a training day. Do you leave and:
a look for the bulletin board? **Go to 12**
b walk to the training rooms? **Go to 3**

5 You need a permit to work to begin so you look for the shift manager. **Go to 21**

6 You guess your shift is drinking tea in the tearoom. Do you:
a go and drink tea with them? **Go to 10**
b start work to make up time? **Go to 5**
c get a snack from the vending machine? **Go to 19**

7 You learnt a lot in health and safety training. Well done! Your shift manager arrives last at the assembly point and is very embarrassed. Finish or start again? **Go to 1**

8 You go in quietly. The subject is working at height, the wrong training. Do you:
a put your hand up to leave? **Go to 20**
b exit quietly at the back? **Go to 9**

9 You walk along the corridor and see a spillage. Do you:
a continue because you are late? **Go to 14**
b stop and clean it up? **Go to 18**

10 You get to the tearoom, but it is empty. Do you:
a go to the canteen? **Go to 16**
b check out the smoking area? **Go to 3**

11 You look through the door of the training room and see your co-workers. Do you:
a knock and enter? **Go to 20**
b walk into the room? **Go to 8**

12 At the noticeboard you read the news about ZemTeQ's football team. A big sign says: 'Training Today'. You go the training block. **Go to 11**

13 Suddenly the fire bell rings. Do you:
a know what to do and where to go? **Go to 7**
b need time to think? **Go to 25**

14 You see some spillage signs and put them up. You then go to room 16. **Go to 13**

15 You go into the room. It's a fire safety lecture. Great! You only missed the introduction. **Go to 17**

16 Nobody is at the canteen. A notice says 'Training Today'. Your shift manager will be furious. Do you:
a go and search in the workshops? **Go to 2**
b look around the new admin block? **Go to 11**

17 You learn about the different types of fire extinguishers. **Go to 13**

18 Your boss sees you with the mop. 'Well done!' he says, 'I'm going to nominate you employee of the month to win a car'. As you are late, do you:
a give him the mop and run off? **Go to 22**
b shake hands, give your name and run to room 16? **Go to 15**

19 You put your money in the vending machine, but nothing comes out. You are cross. Do you:
a go to the tearoom? **Go to 10**
b call your friend to calm down? **Go to 4**

20 The trainer is annoyed. He asks your name and tells you to go to room 16. Do you:
a leave, turn left, then right? **Go to 23**
b leave, turn right, left, then right? **Go to 9**

21 You meet your friend Jimmy and talk about football. Then he mentions the training. **Go to 11**

22 You are concerned about the hazards of the spillage, and so is your shift manager. **Go to 14**

23 You are lost in the new training block. You text your friend, Mike, for help. **Go to 24**

24 Mike's in health and safety training. He says it's really interesting. You text each other about the football on TV last night. Next, do you:
a carry on texting? **Go to 4**
b go for a coffee? **Go to 10**

25 You should pay attention in health and safety training. It can save your life. **Go to 1**

▶ **3** **Focus on words**

Find words similar to 1–8 in the maze text. With a partner, try asking questions using these words.

1 hallway   **2** notice   **3** colleague   **4** meeting point
5 alarm   **6** cross   **7** building   **8** worried

6 Numbers and units

Objective: To review language for numbers and units of measurement and practise using them correctly.

▶ 1 Say the numbers

With a partner, take it in turns to say the numbers below. Check you agree with the pronunciation of each number.

1	3	**5**	200	**9**	500,000	**13**	21.45 kg	**17**	8:58 a.m.	**21**	−4¼ =
2	14	**6**	1,300	**10**	¾ million	**14**	3½ hrs	**18**	6 cm ÷ 2 cm =
3	78	**7**	7,498	**11**	678,311	**15**	95%	**19**	1:15 p.m.
4	158	**8**	23,000	**12**	9.123	**16**	3 m² x 2 m²	**20**	95¼

▶ 2 Spot the difference

Student A should look at this picture and Student B should turn to the picture on page 135. The numbers and units are similar, but there are a few differences. Take it in turns to describe your picture and find the differences.

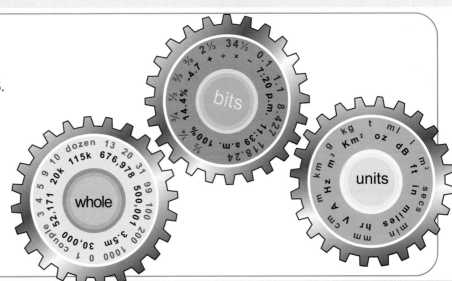

▶ 3 Quiz the class

a In groups, guess the answers to the questions below. Remember to use units!

b Write similar questions of your own for a class quiz.

How high is Everest?	_____
How long is the Nile?	_____
Approximately how heavy is an adult African elephant?	_____
How wide is China?	_____
How old is Paris?	_____
How many countries are there in the world?	_____
How much does an English stamp cost?	_____

Objective: To practise language for greetings and informal social chat in the workplace.

▶ **1** ⓪ **1:3 Listen and write**

Listen to the conversation between Richard and one of his students and write the missing words and phrases below.

J 1 _____, are you here for the course?

R Yes, I am. I'm the teacher. 2 _____ Richard.

J 3 _____, Richard, I'm Jimmy. Do you work in the health and safety department at ZemTeQ, or are you from another company?

R I'm from another training company, but 4 _____ at ZemTeQ for years. Which 5 _____ do you work in, Jimmy?

J I'm a new 6 _____ in health and safety. I've been at ZemTeQ for two weeks now. I like the work, but I don't like the early mornings.

R What about the holidays and other 7 _____? I thought ZemTeQ was pretty good.

J Yeah, it's OK. I get three weeks vacation a year. So, Richard, 8 _____ your e-mail address to ask any questions about the course?

R Sure, Jimmy, it's devonshire@hnstraining.com. 9 _____, I've got to go and get ready. 10 _____, Jimmy.

A teacher and a student meet for the first time before a class. They get to know each other with some small talk and ask each other some informal questions, but nothing too personal.

▶ **2** **Find and choose**

Write 1–10 next to the words and phrases that have a similar meaning to those from the conversation. Use some numbers more than once.

a	hi	____	**k**	area	____
b	apprentice	____	**l**	student	____
c	section	____	**m**	you can call me	____
d	division	____	**n**	perks	____
e	how do you do	____	**o**	I've been	____
f	well	____	**p**	anyhow	____
g	good morning	____	**q**	could I ask for	____
h	I'm	____	**r**	I've been employed	____
i	extras	____	**s**	a pleasure to meet you	____
j	will you let me have	____	**t**	goodbye	____

Two customers are in a queue in a bank. The line is moving very slowly. One thinks he recognizes the other customer from somewhere. He starts a conversation with the other customer and tries to find out where he knows him from.

▶ **3** **Read and speak**

With a partner, act out the conversation several times using different words and phrases from Task 2.

Two workers start a new job on the same day. They are strangers, but know they are waiting for the same supervisor to collect them from the waiting room. They also know they are going to be working together so they should get to know each other.

▶ **4** **Read and write**

a Read the scenarios opposite and choose one.

b With a partner, write out the conversation using words and phrases from Tasks 1 and 2.

c Practise your conversation and then perform it for the class.

Activate your vocabulary
Go to page 152.

Hazards and risk assessment

1 | Risk assessment

Objectives: To discuss risk assessment. To practise listening for specific words and reading for specific information.

▶ 1 Read and speak

Discuss the questions below with a partner and then as a class.

1 What dangers can you see in the classroom?
2 Is there a good chance or a slim chance of these dangers causing accidents in the classroom?
3 How many hazards or dangers are in your work area?
4 What is the chance or risk level of you having an accident with these dangers at work?
5 How can you lower the risk for these hazards?

▶ 2 ⓹ 1:4 Listen and write

You are going to listen to Richard giving a lecture which introduces risk assessment. Listen and write the missing words and phrases.

Good morning. I hope you are all well and ready to look at some health and safety. Today, we will talk about
1 _____, which helps us know what to do to stop accidents happening. Risk assessment helps
us to think about **2** _____ hazards and **3** _____ risks. Let me clarify a few terms here.
A **4** _____ is something that **5** _____, for example, a chemical or using a
ladder. A **6** _____ is the chance a person is harmed or injured by the hazard.
Generally, we do a risk assessment by going through the following steps:
First, look for the hazards that might cause serious harm or injury to people. For example,
7 _____, fire, chemicals, moving machinery, working at **8** _____,
vehicles, electricity, dust and fumes, **9** _____, noise and poor lighting. That's just to name a few.
So you need to be thinking, thinking, thinking.
Next, decide who is at risk and how they are at risk. There are always more people than you think: trainees,
cleaners, the boss. Stop and think before you do the job.
After this, **10** _____ the risk level, usually written as low, medium or high risk. Decide if
precautions are adequate or if more should be done, for example, by eliminating the job,
11 _____ the item, changing the work method, reducing **12** _____ time, adding
engineering controls, using good housekeeping, using safe systems of work, doing extra training, using
13 _____, and so on.
The next step is to **14** _____ of the risk assessment. Other people will want to
look at your decisions. You might want to look at what you wrote a year ago, so you can do the job better now.
Finally, **15** _____ the risk assessment after some time, or if there is an accident or incident, or even
a change in the machine being used to do a job.

▶ 3 Read and answer

Read through the lecture and answer the questions below.

1 You are the only person who needs to read the risk assessment in the future.
  True or false?
2 The risk assessment steps can be done in any order.
  True or false?
3 'And so on' is an important precaution. True or false?
4 What is the difference between a hazard and a risk?
5 How long is the risk assessment valid for?
6 What should you do if the precautions are insufficient?
7 What do you think is the most important step? Why?
8 What is different about risk assessment in your company or section?

▶ 4 Odd one out

Look at each group of words on page 135. Find the 'different' word in each group. Say why you think it is different.

Objectives: To become more familiar with vocabulary on a risk assessment form. To focus on stress patterns.

A company will often have a standard form to fill in for risk assessment. Each job needs one of these for you and other workers to use to think about the hazards for that job.

▶ 1 Check and fill

Check the form below for new words as a class. Fill in the form for a job/task you do often and explain it to another student.

H&S Risk Assessment	ZemTeQ # 427/b	Date:

Job/Task:

Worker name	Dept./section
Worker #	Tel.
Position	E-mail

Main hazards ** tick the correct boxes for the job*

A EQUIPMENT	E ELECTRICITY		K ENVIRONMENTAL	
entanglement	☐ fixed installation		☐ noise	☐
friction/abrasion	☐ portable tools/equipment	☐	vibration	☐
cutting	**F CHEMICALS**		light	☐
shearing	☐ dust/fumes/gas		☐ humidity	☐
stabbing/puncturing	☐ toxic		☐ ventilation	☐
impact	☐ irritant		☐ temperature	☐
pressure	☐ corrosive		☐ overcrowding	☐
ejection of part	☐ carcinogenic		**L WORKER**	
display equipment	**G FIRE/EXPLOSION**		unsuitable for job	☐
hand tools	☐ flammable material		☐ long hours	☐
B TRANSPORT	explosion		☐ high work rate	☐
work vehicles	☐ means of escape		☐ violence	☐
mechanical handling	**H PARTICLES & DUST**		unsafe behaviour	☐
pedestrians	☐ inhalation		☐ stress	☐
C ACCESS	ingestion		☐ young	☐
slips, trips, falls	☐ skin/eye abrasion		**M OTHER**	
falling/moving objects	**I RADIATION**		poor maintenance	☐
obstruction	☐ ionising		☐ no training/info/supervision	☐
work at height	☐ non-ionising	☐		
confined space	**J BIOLOGICAL**			
excavation	☐ bacterial		☐	
D HANDLING	viral		☐	
manual handling	☐ fungal		☐	
mechanical handling	☐			

Risk detail ** write some specific detail about the hazards and risk*

Persons at risk ** list the people **who** are at risk and **how** they are at risk*

Consequences ** give possible injuries as a result of the hazards*

SIGNATURE:

▶ 2 Speak and write

a Ask a partner about a job they do and fill in the details on the risk assessment form on page 136.

b Explain the details of your job to your partner so they can fill in their form.

c Check both forms and discuss the most important ways to prevent accidents.

▶ 3 Pronounce the words

a Write the hazards from the risk assessment form in the correct column in the table on page 136, depending on whether the stress is on the first, second, third or fourth syllable. Check the answers as a class.

b Practise saying the words with a partner.

Objectives: To review and develop vocabulary for describing hazardous situations and control measures.

▶ 1 Solve the crossword

With a partner, work out the answers to the crossword clues, then check as a class. The answers are all on the risk assessment form opposite.

Across

3 Pick up boxes.
5 Truck, car or lorry.
6 _____ on a spillage.
7 Someone working 15-hour shifts works _____ _____.
8 _____ over a cable.
10 Gives you a shock.
11 You work at height with one.
12 Describes breathing in.
13 When hair gets trapped in a machine.
14 Person walking.
15 A very loud _____.
16 Fans and a/c provide _____.
17 Too many people in a place results in _____.

Down

1 A box on the stairs is an _____.
2 100°C is hot.
3 Hammers and saws are _____ _____.
4 Makes you itch and scratch.
9 Bang!
11 You turn it on to see.
12 Eating or drinking.

▶ 2 Identify the control measures

Match the two halves of each control measure in columns A and B. Then in column C, write the crossword answer connected with the control.

A	B	C
1 open	a it in your mouth	1 k ventilation
2 unwind	b petrol in the correct area	
3 lift	c in a pedestrian area	
4 breathe	d at 75 degrees	
5 store	e thick clothes	
6 don't put	f handles before use	
7 take off	g the oil immediately	
8 read	h the walkways	
9 don't park	i a break often	
10 take	j the label first	
11 inspect	k a window	
12 keep	l the load carefully	
13 switch on	m the workers in an area	
14 plug in	n the length you need	
15 place	o items away from the walkways	
16 limit	p earplugs	
17 lean	q an inspected socket	
18 stay in	r light if too dark	
19 mop up	s with a mask	
20 wear	t it short	

▶ 3 Ask and find out

Discuss these questions in small groups.

1 Can you think of other types of control measure to avoid the hazards from Task 1?
2 What types of injuries result from these hazards?
3 Which hazards are most common in your section?

▶ 4 Walk and talk

a In groups, ask each other the questions on page 137 and mark how many people answered yes or no.
b Report what you discovered to the class.

Objective: To practise describing and categorizing different types of hazards and discussing risk levels and precautions.

This is a picture of ZemTeQ's site before health and safety was a priority. As you can see, there were lots of problems and injuries as a result. How many dangers can you find?

▶ **1** **Find and discuss**

a Find the items below in the picture.

1 ladder
2 mop
3 chainsaw
4 steps
5 entrance
6 forklift
7 sign
8 scaffold
9 vehicle
10 crane
11 tank
12 hose
13 extinguisher
14 leak
15 animal
16 hole
17 tool
18 light
19 container

b What else do you see? With a partner, talk about the contents of the picture for 3–4 minutes.

▶ **2** **Remember and write**

a Close the book and talk about what you remember from the picture in groups.
b Make a list of the hazards you identified.

▶ **3** **Unscramble and count**

a Unscramble the words and phrases to find the main site hazard types.

1 lhvceie syfeat   *vehicle safety*   _I_

2 teorh ahsazdr   _____ ___

3 orpo menaniaentc   _____ ___

4 rognikw ta igtheh   _____ ___

5 nclmaceaih lghdnani _____ ___

6 lunaam ilhdgnna   _____

7 mcchaile ftayes   _____

8 ifer atefys   _____

9 eectrcilla afseyt   _____

10 nespeaidrt fsatey   _____

b Count how many hazards there are of each type in the picture.

▶ 5 Find and talk

a Find 23 verbs in the wordsearch.

b Describe the picture using the verbs below and the hazard types (1–10) from Task 3.

H	S	H	R	S	L	Z	B	J	K	F	R
M	T	M	P	G	L	Z	P	A	L	M	G
E	I	W	I	L	B	E	E	C	G	F	B
E	N	D	G	I	J	L	E	W	B	A	P
R	G	A	X	C	A	L	Y	P	E	L	K
Q	I	S	F	P	A	R	K	N	N	L	Z
X	R	P	C	S	R	C	A	C	D	C	E
Z	U	H	F	A	W	E	Y	L	I	F	T
A	Z	Y	C	S	L	C	R	O	S	S	B
J	S	X	Z	C	D	R	O	P	C	R	S
O	S	I	B	F	W	D	R	O	W	N	U
S	S	A	I	K	W	R	U	N	J	T	M
J	L	T	T	T	R	I	P	K	U	I	U
E	I	E	E	E	Z	Q	N	O	L	N	K
R	P	C	S	P	P	U	N	I	T	X	Z
V	R	N	A	X	V	A	D	H	H	Z	L
C	W	N	B	T	E	A	J	U	R	N	M
U	S	I	W	L	C	X	B	Y	O	I	O
G	M	P	P	F	P	H	R	U	W	F	P
Q	M	W	S	E	C	L	I	M	B	K	A
V	O	M	A	X	P	A	I	N	T	F	X

▶ 4 Think and talk

Think about your job and your section. Now read the questions below and discuss your answers with a partner. Share your ideas with the class.

What hazards do you face in your job?

What hazard type are these from the list (1–10) in Task 3?

What is the level of risk: low, medium or high?

What precautions or controls can you use to prevent accidents from these hazards?

Objective: To understand terms for describing trends and practise talking about trends, graphs and statistics.

Every worker needs to use charts, graphs and tables to record change in the workplace. This could be the number of workers, pay per hour, absenteeism, the temperature of a furnace, output per day or even cups of tea per day. Health and safety needs accurate communication of these changes.

▶ **1** ⊚ **1:5 Listen and draw**

Listen to the teacher describe Jimmy's levels of happiness during the week. Draw a graph opposite to illustrate Jimmy's week.

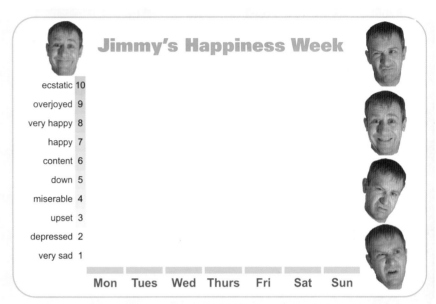

▶ **2** ⊚ **1:6 Listen and write**

Listen again to the teacher describing Jimmy's week and write the missing words.

Jimmy started the week with a score of six because he felt OK after the weekend and a family meal. His happiness level **1** _____ to a four on Monday, because it was Monday. It **2** _____ to nine on Tuesday, after he was given a surprise promotion, but **3** _____ to two the next day, when his boss said it was a mistake. The following day, his mood **4** _____ to seven as he spent time with his friends in a restaurant. On Friday, it **5** _____ at seven because it was Friday and the end of the working week. Also, he had plans to go fishing at the weekend. His mood **6** _____ to two the next day as he sat fishing all day on the river and caught nothing. His happiness level **7** _____ to ten on Sunday because he caught a huge fish then cooked it on his BBQ for his friends, and then had an early night and slept well.

▶ **3** **Find the verbs**

a Work with a partner. Student A go to page 137, Student B go to page 138. Swap verbs to complete your grid.

b Using the verbs in your grid, complete the table next to it.

▶ **4** **Talk about trends**

a Use the language from this lesson to draw a graph about the one of the subjects below.

1 rainfall this year
2 accidents this year in your company
3 your happiness last week

4 your sports team's performance this year
5 employee numbers at your company over the last ten years
6 you decide

b Present your graph to the class and describe the trends that it shows.

6 | Opinions

At work, we need to give our opinions every day. This is true in the meeting room, workshop and even the canteen. We tell the listener how strong our opinions are using special phrases, as well as our voice, body language and facial expressions.

▶ 1 Match and write

The percentage bar below shows how strongly you feel (+) or don't feel (-) about something. Match the phrases (a–k) with the facial expressions and body language (1–11) and then to the number range (-100% to +100%) below.

a I'm not really sure if ___ 0%   **e** I definitely don't think ___ ___   **i** I don't believe ___ ___

b I really doubt ___ ___   **f** I'm convinced ___ ___   **j** I kind of reckon ___ ___

c I don't really feel ___ ___   **g** I guess ___ ___   **k** I'm pretty positive ___ ___

d I'm almost certain ___ ___   **h** I'm inclined not to say ___ ___

1	2	3	4	5	6	7	8	9	10	11

-100%	-80%	-60%	-40%	-20%	0%	20%	40%	60%	80%	100%

▶ 2 Decide and discuss

a Read and check the sentences below for unknown words.

1 ___ We should all get a 10% pay rise.

2 ___ Working at height causes most accidents at work.

3 ___ Night shift are lazier than day shift.

4 ___ Left-handed people have more accidents.

5 ___ Japanese cars are the best.

6 ___ All children should learn to swim.

7 ___ Hard work is the best way to a promotion.

8 ___ No one can do CPR in this room.

9 ___ All of us will do our English homework.

10 ___ People should work until they are 70.

b Use the phrases from Task 1 to complete the sentences, according to your opinions. Discuss your opinions with a partner and then as a class. Remember to give reasons for your opinions.

▶ 3 Speak and decide

Read the situations and discuss your opinions with a partner.

Situation 1	You walk into a work area and find a worker unconscious near an electric cable.

Situation 3	A friend tells you to move a container of caustic solution. What do you do?

Situation 2	Your shift manager asks you to do a new job. You don't know what PPE to use.

Situation 4	It's raining and windy and you need to work at height. What do you do?

▶ 4 Take part in a meeting

a In small groups, discuss the items on the meeting agenda on page 137.

b Make a decision about each item and then explain your ideas to the class.

7 | Small talk: 'How are you?'

Objective: To become more familiar with useful vocabulary and phrases for making small talk in English.

People like to talk about the recent past to make small talk after they ask each other how they are.

▶ 1 🔊 1:7 Listen and write

Listen to the conversation and write the missing words and phrases below.

R Good morning, Jimmy. **1** _____ ?

J Oh, hi, Richard. I'm **2** _____. And you?

R **3** _____. Did you have a good week?

J Yes, I learnt a lot last week, you know, new people, new jobs. You?

R A difficult week. We had some **4** _____. New computers, then the car **5** _____, but the weekend was good. How was your weekend?

J **6** _____. We went shopping and had a family meal at my house. I studied a lot for this new job and watched a few movies.

R Did you go to that new shopping mall out of town?

J Yes, it's **7** _____. I went to about 30 or 40 shops. I was so tired ... and broke. Oh, by the way, thanks for answering my e-mail questions.

R **8** _____. Anytime. Are you enjoying the course?

J **9** _____. So what are we doing this week?

R Aha, surprise. I'll **10** _____.

A line manager meets one of his workers on the first morning after the weekend. They start to chat and ask how each other's weekend went and what they did.

A couple of friends bump into each other in the canteen and start chatting. They haven't seen each other since before their vacations, so they ask in turn about how their holidays went and what sort of things they got up to.

▶ 2 Find and choose

Write 1–10 next to the words and phrases that have a similar meaning to those from the conversation. Use some numbers more than once.

a full-on ____
b let you know in a while ____
c you're welcome ____
d setbacks ____
e conked out ____
f fine ____
g how are things ____
h so-so ____
i enormous ____
j without a doubt ____
k vast ____
l rushed off my feet ____
m non-stop ____
n packed in ____
o for sure ____
p hiccups ____
q everything OK ____
r massive ____
s OK ____

▶ 3 Read and speak

With a partner, act out the conversation several times using different words and phrases from Task 2.

▶ 4 Read and write

a Read the situations opposite and choose one.
b With a partner, write a conversation using words and phrases from Tasks 1 and 2.
c Practise your conversation and then perform it for the class.

You see the English teacher walking to work after the weekend. You stop and give them a lift and chat about what you have done over the weekend.

Activate your vocabulary
Go to page 152.

Personal Protective Equipment (PPE)

3

1 Parts of the body

Objectives: To review vocabulary for parts of the body and PPE. To practise listening for specific information.

▶ 1 Find, match and label

Find 25 parts of the body in the wordsearch. Use them to label the picture below.

D	Z	T	Q	Y	L	E	G	K	W	R	I	S	T	U	O	B	H
Y	H	U	E	Y	E	F	I	N	G	E	R	T	F	B	E	R	A
N	T	F	S	T	O	M	A	C	H	T	L	M	F	L	M	A	I
O	F	R	O	N	H	A	N	D	S	C	R	B	K	N	O	I	R
S	A	Z	E	O	E	F	E	E	N	A	R	N	O	W	U	N	B
E	H	E	A	R	T	C	H	D	H	E	A	D	D	W	T	B	O
M	N	K	G	B	A	C	K	H	R	L	U	N	G	F	H	Y	N
K	T	O	E	S	H	O	U	L	D	E	R	T	H	R	O	A	T

▶ 2 Name the items

Which items of PPE can you see in the signs?

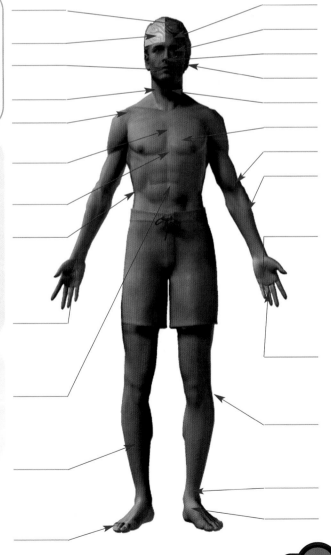

▶ 3 ⊙ 1:8 Listen and answer

Listen to the lecture and mark if the sentences below are true (T) or false (F).

1 Richard said PPE stands for Personal Protective Equipment. _____

2 Richard said elbows are the most important body part to protect. _____

3 We need to choose stylish gloves. _____

4 Your PPE choice only saves **your** life. _____

5 You must use the most expensive PPE. _____

▶ 4 ⊙ 1:9 Listen and write

Listen to the lecture again and complete the table on page 138 with all the main body areas which require PPE, the hazards they face and the type of PPE used to protect them.
(… suggests more information is required.)

2 PPE vocabulary

Objective: To broaden vocabulary for talking about PPE and practise talking about PPE use and misuse.

▶ 1 Walk and talk

Complete the questionnaire by ticking the correct column for each question. Then ask the other students in the class. See how many ticks you have in each column.

	Never	Sometimes	Always
1 Do you put on your hard hat first on site?			
2 Is sunscreen or barrier cream important for you outside?			
3 Have you ever worn resistant gloves or splash-proof leggings?			
4 Are steel-capped boots necessary in your section?			
5 Do you always wear earplugs or defenders in a noisy area?			
6 Do you need high-visibility gear in your section?			
7 Do you read warning signs on site?			
8 How often do you replace damaged PPE?			

▶ 2 Match and ask

a Complete the questions using the verbs in the box. Sometimes more than one answer is possible.

1   Where do you _____ chemicals such as bleach at home? ☐
2   Why is it important to store and _____ PPE carefully? ☐
3   Do you _____ screws with an electric screwdriver or a normal one? ☐
4   Do you _____ your shoes when you go into your house? ☐
5   Do you _____ the oil level in your car every week? ☐
6   Can you think or _____ when there is a lot of noise in the background? ☐
7   Do you _____ clothes before you buy them? ☐
8   How well do you _____ your tools? ☐
9   Do you _____ your jacket or shoes first when you leave home? ☐
10 How many incidents do you _____ each year? ☐
11 How often do you _____ your car with a new one? ☐
12 Do you ever _____ on wet or icy surfaces at work? ☐
13 Does your boss _____? ☐
14 Do you _____ your right or left shoe first when you come home? ☐
15 How do you _____ your body at work? ☐
16 How can you _____ fire at home? ☐

> check   prevent   put on   slip   protect   take off   shout   maintain   store
> try on   remove   report   concentrate   look after   tighten   replace

b Use the questions to interview another student.

3 Identify and describe

a With a partner, label the PPE items and hazards in the picture using the words on page 139.

b Describe what is happening in the picture. Try using words from Task 1 when speaking.

Example: *Someone is tightening his belt. Another man's hard hat is back to front. The earplugs are next to the ear defenders.*

PPE dilemma maze

Objective: To practise careful reading and listening in order to make decisions and evaluations about PPE needs and requirements.

► 1 Read, listen and decide

Work in groups of three. Take it in turns to read out the situation in each step and decide which way to go. Find your way out of the maze by answering correctly.

Situation: The health and safety boss has just had a meeting with Jimmy about checking a building site for problems. He wants Jimmy to look closely at the PPE situation on site and write a report with any recommendations for improvement.

1 Jimmy comes out of the meeting a little confused. He knows there are lots of important things to think about with PPE. He makes a list:
  a Store and maintain properly, don't write name of owner on PPE.   **Go to 23**
  b PPE should suit the purpose, report damaged PPE, maintain properly.   **Go to 7**
  c PPE reduces risk, must be tough, replace damaged PPE.   **Go to 5**

2 You know this number is not in the puzzle, so go back to the number you were looking at. Don't cheat!

3 Jimmy is seriously injured and goes to hospital for two weeks. On his return, the health and safety boss asks him to start the report again, saying why he was injured.   **Go to 1**

4 He checks the sign and is happy with it. He then selects his PPE before going on the building site:
  a helmet, boots, goggles, earplugs, etc.   **Go to 18**
  b helmet, high-visibility clothing, gloves, etc.   **Go to 6**

5 He thinks about worker information for PPE and decides:
  a to put a PPE instruction sheet on the wall.   **Go to 14**
  b not to leave instructions as everyone's had training.   **Go to 10**

6 A brick drops on him. He thinks his helmet might have a dent or scratch. Another brick drops, so he:
  a turns his helmet around to see where the bricks are falling from.   **Go to 17**
  b takes off his helmet and replaces it in the hut.   **Go to 16**
  c tightens the helmet strap and looks up to see the source of the bricks. **Go to 3**

7 Jimmy goes across the site to check on the building of the new workshop. He goes in the hut and checks the helmets. He puts a sign up next to the helmets that reads:
  a Snug strap – not tight. Do not drop, check for damage.   **Go to 4**
  b Do not tilt, do not write your name, look after and clean.   **Go to 13**
  c No cap under helmet, no cigarettes under helmet, write your name on helmet.   **Go to 11**

8 His PPE is not correct. There is a loose cable near a puddle which he walks towards.   **Go to 3**

9 He goes into an area with welding. It is dusty with some oil spills. He changes his footwear to:
  a spats and clogs, as they will be fine.   **Go to 8**
  b clogs, as they are the most comfortable.   **Go to 18**
  c splash-proof leggings (for the oil spills).   **Go to 3**
  d safety trainers, as they are light and comfortable.   **Go to 11**
  e steel-capped boots with non-slip soles and spats (to be careful).   **Go to 15**

10 He wonders if the PPE should be on the table or in the cabinet.
  a He recommends a cabinet or special area.   **Go to 5**
  b He thinks it is OK on the table, as it is easier for access.   **Go to 18**

11 A worker tells him he has done something wrong, so he looks at the sign again.   **Go to 4**

12 After getting his gear on, he thinks that maybe he has forgotten something. He goes outside.   **Go to 8**

13 The PPE sign looks good, but he needs to check the PPE for damage.
  a He asks the first worker who comes through the door if any items are damaged.   **Go to 18**
  b He checks everything himself, even though it takes hours.   **Go to 9**

14 A worker with long hair asks Jimmy what to do about it. He suggests:
  a using a hairnet under his helmet to prevent entanglement.   **Go to 21**
  b tucking the hair under the helmet.   **Go to 12**
  c using a cap under the helmet to keep the hair together.   **Go to 18**

15 This area is dusty and the ground has many obstacles, so he:
  a puts on a disposable dust mask.   **Go to 19**
  b tries on a half-mask respirator.   **Go to 16**
  c wears nothing, as there isn't much dust.   **Go to 3**
  d puts on a full-face respirator. **Go to 18**

16 His strap is loose and will not tighten, so he:
  a uses tape to repair the strap. **Go to 20**
  b takes off the item to fix on site. **Go to 3**

17 He can't see the workers above him, so he:
  a turns the helmet back to front.   **Go to 18**
  b takes off his helmet to see better.   **Go to 3**
  c realizes his helmet doesn't fit. **Go to 16**

18 The health and safety manager sees him and gets very angry. Jimmy must start again and use correct PPE.   **Go to 1**

19 Jimmy wore most of the correct PPE for the job and the health and safety manager is very happy with the report. Review all the information to see what you agree or disagree with.

20 The health and safety manager sees him and starts shouting angrily. Jimmy must start again and use correct PPE. **Go to 1**

21 The weather changes, it's going to be very hot and sunny. Jimmy needs to work outside all day. He decides to:
  a wear sunglasses.   **Go to 22**
  b put on sunscreen.   **Go to 12**

22 It's very dark with the glasses on and he clearly can't wear them on a building site. He decides to:
  a return to change into different gear.   **Go to 14**
  b carry on, as they will be OK after five minutes.   **Go to 3**
  c take them off, as he can manage without them.   **Go to 12**

23 It starts raining again and he needs to be outside to check some scaffolding, so he:
  a grabs some all weather clothing.   **Go to 24**
  b takes some non-slip boots and high-visibility gear.   **Go to 25**

24 It's very noisy here and his ears hurt. He:
  a doesn't put on ear protection, as he must talk to some people on site.   **Go to 26**
  b uses some defenders to protect his ears.   **Go to 27**

25 There is a lot of sharp glass and metal here and he needs to protect his hands. He decides to put on:
  a resistant gloves with barrier cream.   **Go to 26**
  b protective gloves with sleeves.   **Go to 27**

26 He feels a little uncomfortable with his PPE and cannot concentrate on what he is doing. He decides to:
  a take off one item.   **Go to 20**
  b go back to the hut to check his PPE.   **Go to 23**

27 He notices the last maintenance date for the PPE was three months ago. He decides to:
  a carry on with what he is doing, as the changing hut is far away.   **Go to 26**
  b go back to the hut to change his PPE.   **Go to 23**

4 Writing e-mails

Objective: To practise writing short, clear e-mails in an appropriate style.

▶ 1 Read and order

It is normal to write e-mails to your boss or people you don't know that are more formal than e-mails to your co-workers or friends. Reorder the words and phrases below from formal to informal.

1 Hi / Dear / Hello / Hey _____

2 Can you call me? / Could you call me please? / Would you mind calling me? /
   Call me _____

3 Cheers / Thanks / Best wishes / Regards _____

▶ 2 Read and reply

a Read Jimmy's e-mail. Is it formal or informal?

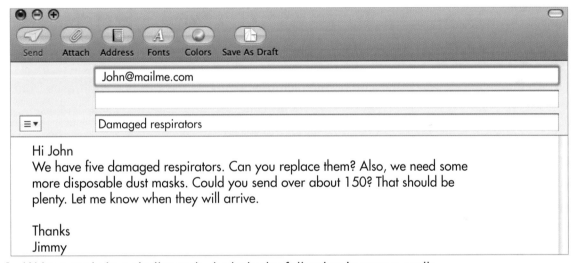

Send Attach Address Fonts Colors Save As Draft

John@mailme.com

Damaged respirators

Hi John
We have five damaged respirators. Can you replace them? Also, we need some more disposable dust masks. Could you send over about 150? That should be plenty. Let me know when they will arrive.

Thanks
Jimmy

b Write a reply in a similar style. Include the following in your e-mail:

• agree to send the respirators, ask what kind he wants
• let Jimmy know how many face masks you can provide (you don't have 150)
• say when you will send them over

▶ 3 Write and swap

Work with a partner (one is A, the other is B). Write e-mails according to the instruction boxes. Exchange sheets after each e-mail.

1 **A:** Ask when the next fire drill is and how the new trainee is getting on.
  B: Give information about the next fire drill (date and time) and the new trainee; ask if he can go on a first-aid training course.

2 **A:** Ask what type of first-aid course (basic first aid or CPR); suggest that other staff members may also need to go on first-aid courses.
  B: Suggest other staff for first-aid courses; give information about how many and what type of courses are needed; complain that staff need better safety goggles.

3 **A:** Agree to provide better goggles. Suggest that B comes to the health and safety meeting next week; give time and date.
  B: Thank A for his help; agree to come to the meeting.

Position and location

Objective: To review prepositions of place and practise describing the location of things.

▶ 1 Unscramble and write

Unscramble the letters to make words and phrases to describe the position of things.

1 ni oftno fo   _in front of_
2 no eht ihgir fo _____
3 ni het ercetn   _____
4 bnidhe   _____
5 ttobmo   _____
6 no hte flet fo   _____
7 ni eweentb   _____
8 beavo   _____
9 lebow   _____
10 pot   _____

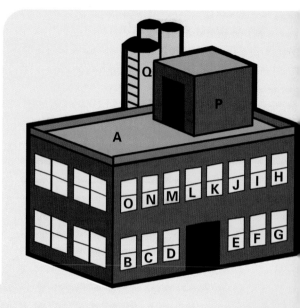

▶ 2 Describe location

a Complete the sentences describing the picture above. Use the words and phrases from Task 1.

1 D is _____ E.
2 N is _____ O.
3 M is _____ L and N.
4 P is _____ I, J and K.
5 P is _____ Q.
6 Q is _____ P.
7 G is _____ H.
8 K is _____ of J and L.
9 B is at the _____ of the building.
10 P is on _____ of the building.

b Make more sentences about the location of the letters on the building.

▶ 3 Read and match

a Jimmy has to check the contents of Plant 4's store cabinet opposite. He gets an e-mail from the supervisor about the contents. Read the e-mail and identify the contents (1–26).

Send Attach Address Fonts Colors Save As Draft

Jimmy@mailme.com

RE: Damaged respirators

Hi Jimmy,

Sorry about the mess in the cabinet. Let me tell you what's there. There's some *hand soap* on the left of the *talc*, which is on the left of the *hard hats*. Below these you can find the *toilet paper*. I think there's some *hand lotion* between the *extinguishers* and the *sunscreen*, which is on the right of the *hand cream*. The *safety gloves* are between the *steel polish* and the *furniture spray*. On the right of the *goggles* you'll find some *barrier cream*, which is above the *toilet bleach*. I think the *defenders* are between the *toilet bleach* and *industrial cleaner*.

I know we keep the *still water* behind the *sparkling drinking water* and the *breathing masks* in front of the *boots*. *Towels* are kept above the *drinking water*. Oh yes, the *steel polish* is on the left of the *concentrated bleach* and the *plasters* are in the centre of the top right shelf. That's between the *antiseptic wipes* and the *hand wipes*.

I know the PPE should not be in there. Sorry. I'll sort it out later. Don't forget football practice on Monday (or is it Tuesday?)

Thanks
Dennis

P.S. I can't remember where the *white spirit* is.
P.P.S. I know the *antiseptic wipes* are above the *extinguishers*.

1 _____	14 _____
2 _____	15 _____
3 _____	16 _____
4 _____	17 _____
5 _____	18 _____
6 _____	19 _____
7 _____	20 _____
8 _____	21 _____
9 _____	22 _____
10 _____	23 _____
11 _____	24 _____
12 _____	25 _____
13 _____	26 _____

b Check you understand the meaning of all the items in the cupboard.

▶ 4 Talk about yourself

With a partner, describe the layout and contents of the following places:

1 your work area   **2** the company site   **3** your house or flat   **4** the car park

Objectives: To learn and use vocabulary for describing the organizational structure of a company section. To practise reading for specific information.

▶ 1 Look and answer

Look at the diagram and answer the questions about the organization structure for Plant 4. Use the underlined phrases in your answers.

1 Who is <u>in charge of</u> whom?
2 Who is <u>under</u> whom?
3 Who is <u>directly responsible to</u> whom?
4 Who <u>runs</u> what?
5 Who <u>answers to</u> whom?
6 Who is <u>responsible for</u> what?

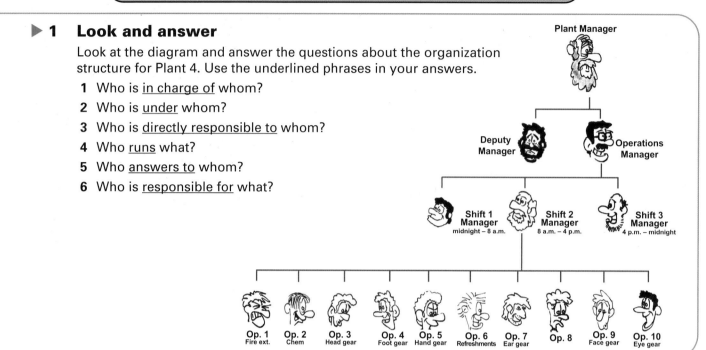

▶ 2 Read and complete

Read the e-mail below and make notes to complete the table on the next page.

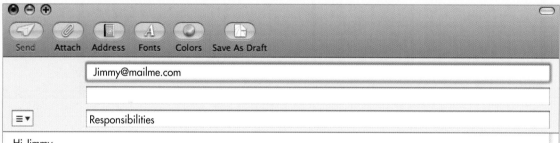

Send   Attach   Address   Fonts   Colors   Save As Draft

Jimmy@mailme.com

Responsibilities

Hi Jimmy,

Here's the info about section responsibilities you asked for.

Rick is not in charge of anybody, but he runs the health and safety inspections and works side by side with Nick. Both are answerable to the big boss for Plant 4, Mick, who is responsible to the GM overseeing all the plants. Nick is in charge of day-to-day production and manages the three shift managers (Ron, John and Don), all of whom give operatives (Op.) news and check that production is OK. All the operatives are responsible for different health and safety equipment checks.

Gaz looks after the equipment to put out fires, so talks to Chaz a lot, who is responsible for checking hazardous substances and where they are stored. Jerry inspects and maintains the goggles and safety specs. Larry checks and replaces dust masks and breathing gear. Vaz maintains and repairs all the gloves, but Daz inspects the helmets, caps and hairnets. Gary is responsible for the coffee and tea around the plant. Baz is in charge of the boots, clogs and safety trainers and is also the designated first-aider, as well as Nick.

Finally, Barry organizes the plugs and defenders, which are especially important in noisy Plant 4. Oh yeah, the vision PPE, hearing PPE and head PPE guys are also responsible for tool checks across the whole plant. The breathing apparatus, sandwich and blaze chaps are in charge of electric equipment checks. The fire-drill team is run by the shoe, mitt and acid blokes. I nearly forgot Harry. He's a trainee and doesn't have any responsibilities except to arrive at work in the morning, which he sometimes doesn't do. John, the Day Shift Manager, is keeping an eye on Harry. That's it. Ask Don, the Evening Shift Manager, if you need more details.

Any questions, let me know.

Cheers
Dennis

Name	Job	Answers to	Responsibilities
	Plant Manager		
	Deputy Manager		
	Operations Manager		
	Shift Manager 1		
	Shift Manager 2		
	Shift Manager 3		
	Operative 1		
	Operative 2		
	Operative 3		
	Operative 4		
	Operative 5		
	Operative 6		
	Operative 7		
	Operative 8		
	Operative 9		
	Operative 10		

▶ 3 Draw and write

a Draw an organization diagram for your plant/section/area/department.

b Explain your diagram to a partner. Your partner should ask questions.

c Write a description of your organization's structure using the phrases in the box below. Don't forget to write what people's responsibilities are.

> … is in charge of … … runs … … oversees … … looks after …
> … is responsible for … … sees to … … answers to … … is under …
> … is directly responsible to …

Objective: Practise social language for giving directions and talking about the weather.

Directions and weather feature in both informal chat and workplace conversation.

▶ 1 ⊙ 1:10 Listen and write

Listen to the conversation and write the missing words and phrases below.

J   Hello, Richard. It's so hot today, isn't it?

R   I prefer it cooler, don't you? How was your week?

J   Pretty good. I tried to find that new fish restaurant on Saturday. Do you know **1** _____?

R   Erm ... yes. It's near that new pool on the other side of town. So, turn left after the lights by the pool. **2** _____ for a mile or so, take the next right and it's **3** _____ the bank and the coffee shop.

J   **4** _____ left, one mile, right, and next to the bank, **5** _____?

R   Yep, **6** _____. It's a great restaurant. I recommend the shellfish.

J   Thanks, Richard. I'm getting a coffee, do you want one? **7** _____.

R   Thank you, Jimmy. Milk and four sugars. Wow, it's **8** _____ today!

J   What will the weather be like this weekend?

R   I **9** _____. I **10** _____ it will be hot again. Anyway, let's get that coffee.

▶ 2 Find and choose

Write 1–10 next to the words and phrases that have a similar meaning to those from the conversation. Use some numbers more than once.

a how can I get to it	____	**k** extremely hot	____
b to recap	____	**l** the way there	____
c in the middle of	____	**m** where it's located	____
d roasting	____	**n** bang on	____
e I'm paying	____	**o** is that correct	____
f go on	____	**p** reckon	____
g scorching	____	**q** keep going	____
h haven't a clue	____	**r** continue	____
i spot on	____	**s** boiling	____
j in a nutshell	____	**t** my shout	____

▶ 3 Read and speak

With a partner, act out the conversation several times using different words and phrases from Task 2.

▶ 4 Read and write

a Read the scenarios opposite and choose one.

b With a partner, write out the conversation using words and phrases from Tasks 1 and 2.

c Practise your conversation and then perform it for the class.

It's your first day in the company and it's lunchtime. You are very hungry and you are lost. Time is running out to get some lunch, so you ask someone for directions, but he starts to talk about the weather.

You are in town and are feeling hungry as it is lunchtime. You don't know the town very well, so you stop a stranger and ask him to recommend a restaurant and then give you some clear directions as to how to get there.

You are going to chat to the teacher about what the weather has been like recently and what will be like this coming week, in your opinion. Include what your plans are for the weekend and each ask directions to a place you want to get to in town, but are not quite sure of how to get there.

You are at a bus stop waiting for a bus that is very late and looks like it will never come. Chat to another passenger about the weather and the late bus.

Your boss sends you on some errands around the plant but you are not sure where the places are. Ask him for clear directions and check them.

Activate your vocabulary
Go to page 152.

Hand-held safety equipment

1 | Hand-held safety equipment

Objectives: To review vocabulary connected with tool safety. To practise listening for gist and specific information.

▶ 1 Choose and compare

Circle the best option to complete each sentence. Compare your answers with another student.

1 To work a power tool, you must
   a wear protective gloves.
   b be over 18.
   c be trained and competent.
   d all of the above.

2 A worker is cutting blocks with a disc-cutter. The hazards are
   a radiation
   b dust in the air
   c skin cancer
   d flying material
   e noise

3 If the guard is missing from a tool, you should
   a make another guard.
   b use the tool quickly.
   c make your friend use it.
   d not use the tool.

4 The head on your hammer is loose. Do you
   a stop work and replace the hammer?
   b use a different heavy tool?
   c use your boot?
   d tell the next shift to do the job?

5 Which should you do?
   a Carry a power tool by the cord.
   b Unplug a tool by pulling the cord.
   c Unplug the tool when not in use.
   d Leave the tool plugged in for the next shift.

▶ 2 Walk and talk

Ask as many people as possible these questions.

1 Which tools do you regularly use?
2 Which is the most dangerous tool, in your opinion?
3 What do you check before you use a power tool?
4 What tool accidents have people had in your company/area/section?

▶ 3 Listen and answer

a ⊚ **1:11** Listen to the lecture and answer the questions.

1 What are the three main controls to prevent injury from hand-held tools?
2 How many tools does Richard mention?

b ⊚ **1:12** Complete the phrases from the lecture. Listen again and check your answers.

1 misuse or poor _____
2 broken _____
3 incorrect use of _____
4 poor _____ handles
5 _____ spanners
6 _____ or _____ hammer-heads
7 poorly _____ tools

▶ 4 ⊚ 1:13 Listen and choose

What did Richard say: a or b?

1 a mechanical involvement ☐
   b mechanical entanglement ☐
2 a frying paste material ☐
   b flying waste material ☐
3 a and harm vibration ☐
   b hand-arm vibration ☐
4 a slipping hazard ☐
   b tripping hazard ☐
5 a implosion risk ☐
   b explosion risk ☐
6 a high nose level ☐
   b high noise level ☐

Objectives: To extend knowledge of vocabulary for describing the shape of objects and tools. To review prepositions of place.

Describing the shape of items is very important in everyday factory-life communication. It could be for a tool, an object or a building that you need, but don't know the name of.

▶ **1 Find and match**

   a Match the shapes (1–12) to their names.

   b Write the adjective form in the third column. (Not all the shape names have an adjective form.)

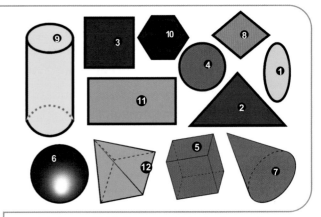

Number	Shape	Adjective
4	circle	circular
	sphere	
	cube	
	cone	
	triangle	
	hexagon	
	oval	
	cylinder	
	diamond	
	rectangle	
	pyramid	
	square	

▶ **2 Describe and draw**

Work with a partner. Student A should look at the picture on page 139. Student B should look at the picture on page 140.
Describe your picture to your partner. They should listen and draw what you describe.

▶ **3 Describe and guess**

Working with a partner again, take it in turns to describe one of the items below. Use some of the shape words in Task 1. Student A should describe the item (without mentioning its name) and Student B should guess the item. Continue with other items at work you are familiar with.

Example: *It's a sphere with circular rings at the top and the bottom. There's a ladder in front of it.*

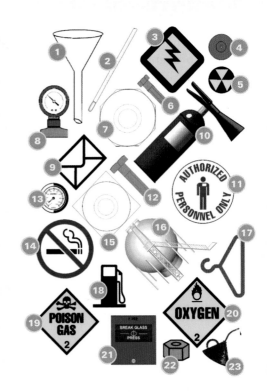

4

Objectives: To learn and organize a lexical set of vocabulary for hand tools. To practise reading and giving definitions.

▶ **1 Find and match**

a Match the words to the pictures.

mole grip	____	awl	____	builder's chisel	____
coping saw	____	allen key	____	pickaxe	____
cable reel	____	file	____	bolt	____
nut	____	chisel	____	craft knife	____
Phillips screwdriver	____	sledgehammer	____	hammer	____
multi-tool	____	flathead screwdriver	____	nail	____
mallet	____	screw	____	crowbar	____
pliers	____	axe	____	handsaw	____
clamp	____	spanner	____	tape measure	____
spirit level	____	wrench	____	oil can	____

b Test each other on the new words by pointing at the pictures and saying the correct words.

▶ **2 Remember and write**

Close your book. With a partner, try to remember as many items as possible from Task 1. List them in groups and explain your grouping to another pair.

▶ **3 Match and describe**

a Read the sentences below. Which tools do they describe?

1 It has a handle. It's pointed and makes small holes in wood. _____

2 It has a rectangular blade and a handle. It cuts medium thick wood. _____

3 It's long and thin and is used to smooth wood. _____

4 It has a thread and a hexagonal or octagonal head. It's used with a nut to secure things. _____

5 It's circular. It stores extension cord. _____

6 It has adjustable jaws and a handle. You use it to grip things. _____

b Make up definitions for some of the other tools. See if your partner can guess the tools you are describing.

Objective: To review vocabulary for hazards and power tools and talk about hazards, training and precautions.

▶ 1 Unscramble and match

What do you think these power tools are called? Unscramble their names and put the picture letter next to the name.

ltei tcerut tile cutter e	rgdenri	uacumv craeeln
anli ung	ceslsdro lirdl	eradsn
erleccit amermh	aws	teha ngu

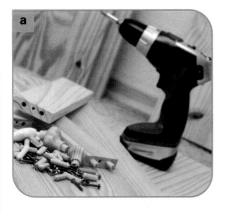

a

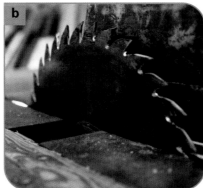

b

c

d

e

f

g

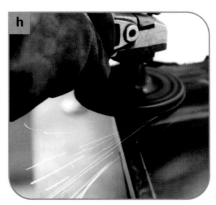

h

i

▶ 2 Discuss with a partner

Discuss the questions below with a partner and feed back to the class your answers and opinions to see if the class agree or not.

1 Of the tools opposite, which three are the most dangerous? Why?

2 Which is the least dangerous tool? Why?

3 Which do carpenters / bricklayers / lathe workers / roofers / scaffolders / plumbers use?

▶ 3 Match the tools with the hazards

a Each tool has many hazards. Write the tool letter (a–i) next to the correct hazard.

mechanical entanglement _____

flying waste material _____

contact with cutting blades _____

hit gas, water and electrical services _____

handling problems because heavy _____

hand-arm vibration _____

trip hazards from cables _____

explosion risk if petrol-driven _____

high noise level _____

dust _____

b With your partner, decide what controls and precautions you would use to prevent injury when using each tool.

▶ 4 Order and speak

a Read the tool inspector's questions below. Put them in the correct places to complete the conversation opposite.

b With a partner, practise reading the conversation.

c Choose other tools and create similar conversations.

Inspector's questions

1 How often do you check it for damage?

2 Where do you store it?

3 Do you repair it if it is broken?

4 How do you use a [tool]?

5 Are you trained to use a [tool]?

6 Is a [tool] suitable for the [job]?

A _____
B Well, first [...], second [...], third [...].
A _____
B Yes, it is appropriate.
A _____
B I check it every time I use it.
A _____
B No, I call maintenance.
A _____
B I keep it in [place].
A _____
B Yes, I learnt to use it [time] ago.

Objectives: To become more familiar with the language and functions of instructions. To practise intensive reading for detailed information.

Safety instructions are a very important part of a tool's user guide or manual. The worker must become familiar with this information before using a tool.

▶ 1 Label and check

a In groups, match the chainsaw labels with the phrases below.

a oil filler cap _____

b front handle _____

c starter trigger cover _____

d stop switch _____

e back handle _____

f hand guard _____

g chain _____

h motor cooling vent _____

i chain bar _____

j throttle trigger _____

b Compare your answers with other groups.

▶ 2 Complete the text

a Read part of the Safety Instruction Leaflet for ZemTeQ's 4x-12 chainsaw.

b Complete the instructions using the words in the box.

> topside   instruction   clamp
> tired   chain   grip   off
> handle   dry   wood   remove
> repaired   use   guard   clean
> stop   putting   before   hearing
> damaged   non-skid
> unstable   objects

1 Should be practical _____ for first-time user.

2 Know how to _____ saw in an emergency.

3 Make sure work area is _____ and get secure footing before start.

4 Store in a _____ secure place with guard fitted when not in use.

5 Wear rubber gloves and _____ footwear, but not loose clothing.

6 Put on safety glasses plus _____ and head protection.

7 Carry chainsaw by front _____, keep finger off switch and guard on.

8 Check for damage _____ each use.

9 Keep the _____ sharp and clean for safer performance.

10 Switch _____ the chain before inspecting.

11 Stay alert, do not use when _____.

12 Get saw _____ by qualified person.

13 Do not operate saw that is _____.

14 _____ chainsaw with both hands and fingers wrapped around handles.

15 Use only underside of the chain bar saw for cutting. Never use _____.

16 _____ against kickback caused by tip contact with wood.

17 Check chain brake for correct operation before _____.

18 Never use in tree, on ladder or other _____ surface.

19 Make sure the wood does not contain nails, screws or other _____.

20 Always switch off before _____ chainsaw down.

21 Secure work with a _____, never use foot to support wood.

22 Clean chainsaw, oil chain, _____ any debris before putting away.

23 Know the limitations, only saw _____.

▶ 3 Sort the instructions

Read the safety instructions again and put the number of each instruction (1–23) beside the correct instruction category below.

a operating instructions _____

b storage instructions _____

c maintenance _____

d PPE _____

▶ 4 Choose a sign

Look at the health and safety signs below. Which would you associate with the chainsaw? Be prepared to explain why to the class. Work in groups.

▶ 5 Make a poster

a In groups, make a poster about a tool your group knows something about. Include:

- a labelled diagram
- operating instructions
- transport instructions
- maintenance instructions
- PPE and storage instructions
- safety signs for the tool
- five questions for the reader

b Put the posters on the wall and circulate with a partner. Make a note of the title of each poster and your answers to the questions on each one. Discuss your answers as a class.

Objective: To become familiar with the terminology on a permit to work form and practise completing this form.

The permit to work is a type of 'safe systems of work' procedure to make sure dangerous work is done safely. This permission is given by authorized staff, who make sure all the precautions are in place. Opposite is ZemTeQ's form. (Your company's form will have some differences.)

▶ 1 Read and match

Read the sections (1–13) of the permit to work form opposite and match them with the section descriptions (a–n) below.

a the exact name of the permission for that task in that area _____

b the signed name of the person responsible for controls before the job starts _____

c a small report of what the job is: why, what, when, how, who, limitations _____

d signature to say all checks done, so work can continue with new workers, and they know the job, hazards and precautions _____

e a unique number given to this permission form and permit _____

f isolations: controls and preventative measures needed before job starts _____

g to say job has been tested, is satisfactory and normal plant work can continue _____

h protective apparatus needed to prevent injury for the job _____

i signature to say work finished and plant ready for testing _____

j signature to say precautions are all in place with date and time duration of permit _____

k the name of the work/task the worker will do _____

l signature to say work to be done, hazards and precautions were explained to the workers _____

m the name of the exact location of the task with area, section and plant number _____

n all dangers existing before job and caused by the job _____

▶ 2 Complete the conversation

a Complete the permit to work conversation between Jimmy and Pete using the questions (a–i) below.

Jimmy's questions

a What's the exact spot?

b Who's doing the acceptance, Dean Pink?

c What does the work involve?

d What protection are you putting on?

e Permit name?

f Billy Black?

g Is Willy White going to do the handing over?

h Who's going to sign for precautions?

i Have you got the code for that pipe job this afternoon?

b Use this information to fill in the correct sections of the permit form.

J Hey, Pete, **1** _____?

P Hi, Jimmy. Yeah. Hold on ... err ... 6x-21/5.

J OK, **2** _____?

P Yep, Willy will take the next shift.

J Got it. **3** _____?

P Oil-Line Check 6x ... I think.

J Good. And **4** _____?

P It's a check on the oil pipeline at the junction for cracks; there's been a drop in pressure.

J Sure, so it's a Line Fault Check. **5** _____?

P Body suit, gloves, goggles. To be sure, we'll take fire equipment. As a precaution, we'll shut down the site and turn off gauges 1–12 and shut off feeder lines 7–15.

J Sounds good. **6** _____?

P Tommy Red and Benny Blue will do precaution checks. So 6th July for two hours: 2 p.m.–4 p.m.

J Cheers. **7** _____?

P Line B7 in Zone K – section 3.

J **8** _____?

P No, he's on holiday. Matty Brown will step in. And Black'll do the handover.

J **9** _____?

P Yep. I need Alfie Green to finish it off, too.

J No problem. Thanks, Pete.

P See you around, Jimmy.

ZemTeQ
Permit to work

1 Permit Title	2 Permit #

3 Job Title

4 Plant ID

5 Work Description

6 Hazard ID

7a Precautions	7b Signatures

8 PPE

9 Authorization

10 Acceptance

11 Extension/Shift Handover

12 Handback

13 Cancellation

▶ 3   **Talk about yourself**

Explain the contents and names of permits to work for specific jobs in your
section. Who signs what? Tell the class about one job form if you have time,
and take questions from the class.

Objective: To become more familiar with useful vocabulary and phrases for describing plans and intentions.

▶ **1** 🎧 **1:14 Listen and write**

Listen to the conversation and write the missing words and phrases below.

J Hello, Richard. Good week?

R Yep, and you? **1** _____ in ZemTeQ's health and safety department?

J OK, a lot of hard work. I'm going to the capital on a report-writing course next week, then I'm **2** _____ some meetings at HQ the week after.

R Busy is better than bored, Jimmy. Are you **3** _____ my course next week?

J **4** _____. I'll send you an e-mail this week. **5** _____ that.

R Don't worry. The week after next I'm going on holiday, so you won't be marked absent then.

J Where are you going on holiday? Somewhere hot?

R No, I'm not. I **6** _____ the hot weather so much. I'm going to go skiing in the mountains up north. Are you going to go on **7** _____ this year, Jimmy?

J I'm **8** _____ my uncle on the coast and go fishing every day. I love it.

R That sounds great. **9** _____ go into the class?

J Sure. **10** _____, Richard. Last week's class was great. I liked ...

▶ **2** **Find and choose**

Write 1–10 next to the words and phrases that have a similar meaning to those from the conversation. Use some numbers more than once.

a how's life ____
b am not fond of ____
c maybe ____
d why don't we ____
e sitting in on ____
f staying with ____
g I'd like to apologize for ____
h a trip ____
i planning on coming to ____
j don't care for ____

k showing my face at ____
l you first ____
m going to show up at ____
n what's happening ____
o possibly ____
p apologies for ____
q let's ____
r how about we ____
s perhaps ____
t vacation ____

▶ **3** **Read and speak**

Act out the conversation in Task 1 two or three times using different words from Task 2.

▶ **4** **Read and write**

a Read the scenarios opposite and choose one.
b With a partner, write out the conversation using words and phrases from Tasks 1 and 2.
c Practise your conversation and then perform it for the class.

You meet a friend in the canteen and discuss rumours you have heard about the big changes that are going to happen in the company.

Two friends and co-workers are trying to organize a special dinner for your section and who is going to do what. They also discuss possible problems that may happen with the plans and what you will do if they occur.

After an inspection by the health and safety inspector, you have a cup of tea and chat about the problems he found in your area. He asks about your future plans to make it safer and makes some suggestions.

It's your first day in the company as one of the new trainees. You introduce yourself to your new section leader, who sits you down and explains his plans for you in your induction week. He will tell you what the likely problems are that you will face in this first week.

Talk to your teacher about your vacation plans and ask him what his are. Say what you are definitely going to do and what you probably won...

Activate your vocabulary
Go to page 152.

Mechanical equipment

1 Mechanical equipment safety

Objectives: To practise listening for gist and for specific words and information. To identify dos and don'ts for dealing with mechanical equipment.

▶ 1 Discuss and share

Discuss the questions below in small groups and share your experiences of machines. The best stories can be shared with the class.

1 Have you had an accident using a machine at home or work? What happened?
2 Why do people have accidents with machines?
3 What control measures can you take to prevent accidents with machines?

1st Control
jigs / jugs
wire mesh / why are machines
gauze / guards
chip systems / trip systems
elastic / plastic
holders / folders

▶ 2 ⦿ 1:15 Listen and answer

Listen to Richard's lecture on mechanical equipment safety and answer the questions below.

1 What four control measures does Richard mention?

i _____ ii _____ iii _____ iv _____

2 What checklist does Richard give at the end?

_____

▶ 3 ⦿ 1:16 Listen and circle

Look at the pairs of words in the circles opposite and listen to the four control measures again.

a Underline the word from each pair that Richard says in the lecture.

b With a partner, discuss what Richard said about each word. Share your ideas with the class.

2nd Control
PPE / BBC
supervisor / supervision
inexperienced / experienced
well lit / we'll eat

3rd Control
working order / walking over
the vices / devices
stop / top
lock-off system / look-up system
resorted / restarted
remove / remote

▶ 4 ⦿ 1:17 Listen and tick

Listen again to Richard's dos and don'ts checklist at the end of his lecture. Which of the following are 'dos' and which are 'don'ts'?

	Do	Don't
1 position guards when in use	☐	☐
2 leave long hair down	☐	☐
3 wear your PPE	☐	☐
4 locate the halt switch	☐	☐
5 use without permission	☐	☐
6 chat to co-workers using machines	☐	☐
7 report faults	☐	☐
8 operate with warning notice	☐	☐
9 put on jewellery	☐	☐
10 keep work area spotless and organized	☐	☐

4th Control
cover / club
pushed / brushed
stop / top
labelled / disabled

▶ 5 Write dos and don'ts

a Think of a machine that you use at work. Write a list of dos and don'ts for people using it.

b Read out your lists to the class. Let them guess which machine it applies to.

Objective: To extend knowledge of vocabulary for describing different types of hazard and practise speaking about mechanical hazards in the workplace.

▶ **1   Find the hazards**

How many different hazard words or phrases for mechanical equipment can you find in the wordsearch below?

E	L	E	C	T	R	O	C	U	T	I	O	N	L	O	U	D	N	O	I	S	E	N	C	U
F	J	S	O	O	E	S	S	R	C	N	F	E	N	T	A	N	G	L	E	M	E	N	T	F
V	V	N	Y	S	E	N	T	R	A	P	M	E	N	T	K	C	R	E	S	K	C	I	Y	G
Y	R	Q	Q	A	I	B	I	L	O	D	R	S	H	A	R	P	E	D	G	E	S	M	I	I
M	V	I	B	R	A	T	I	O	N	P	M	H	O	T	S	U	R	F	A	C	E	V	N	M
E	J	E	C	T	E	D	P	A	R	T	S	O	G	K	E	I	C	E	F	L	A	F	D	S

▶ **2   Match the definitions**

Read the definitions below. What type of hazards are they describing? Write the correct word from the wordsearch next to each one.

1

This is a hazard that occurs through contact with cutting devices or other machine parts. It can result in cuts and even loss of body parts.

2

This is a hazard caused by movement. It can be long-term constant movement or the violent shaking of a machine. It can cause 'white finger' and other HAVs (hand-arm vibrations).

3

This is a hazard caused by a sharp component of a machine or other material flying off a machine. It can cause stabbing or puncturing injuries.

4

This is a hazard if machines are not properly sound-insulated. It can lead to loss of hearing.

5

This hazard is caused by revolving parts of a machine. Loose materials, hair or clothes can be gripped by the machinery.

6

When this happens, a worker is trapped or crushed between a moving part of a machine and a fixed structure.

7

This hazard may occur when workers are in contact with electricity from machines that are poorly insulated and maintained. It can lead to shocks, burns and wounds.

8

This is a hazard when machine surfaces have a high working temperature, or are poorly ventilated and become overheated. It can lead to burns.

▶ **3   Talk about hazards**

With a partner, discuss the mechanical hazards that you can see in the picture on page 139.

Objective: To review vocabulary for PPE and hazards and practise describing prohibition, hazard warning and mandatory signs.

▶ 1 Make sentences

Match the correct sentence halves to make imperative sentences.

a	Look out	___	**1**	the taps running.	*hazard warning*
b	Always wear	___	**2**	forklift trucks.	
c	Never eat or drink	___	**3**	the lift/elevator.	
d	Make sure you lock	___	**4**	in the workshop.	
e	You must not leave	___	**5**	electric shock risk!	
f	Beware of	___	**6**	correct PPE.	
g	Do not use	___	**7**	the store after use.	
h	You must fasten	___	**8**	for spills.	
i	Danger –	___	**9**	your seat belt.	

▶ 2 Look and decide

Look at the different types of signs below. What type of signs would be used to illustrate the sentences from Task 1? Write your answers in the spaces provided in Task 1.

 prohibition

 hazard warning

 mandatory

▶ 3 Spot the difference

Work in groups. Group A should look at the picture opposite. Group B should look at the picture on page 140.

a In groups, discuss what each sign means. Make a sentence for each sign, e.g., *This sign means danger – shallow water.*

b With a partner, describe each sign and find the differences between the two pictures. Do not show your picture to your partner.

▶ 4 My work area signs

Draw the signs that are in your work area and take it in turns to present them to the class. Explain what the signs mean and why they are there.

Objective: To review safety sign language and discuss hazards and the prevention of accidents.

▶ **1 Look and chat**

Look at the *must do* signs, *must not* signs and the *hazard* signs and discuss what they are for. Work in small groups, then share your ideas as a class.

▶ **2 Look and discuss**

Work in groups and answer the questions for each cartoon. Check and discuss as a class when you have all finished and try to reach a consensus.

Accident-prone Andy
a Name the items in the cartoon.
b What hazards can you see?
c What happened?
d What caused it?
e How would you prevent it?
f What signs would you put where?

Speedfreak Steve
a Name the items in the cartoon.
b What hazards can you see?
c What happened?
d What caused it?
e How would you prevent it?
f What signs would you put where?

Jumping Julian
a Name the items in the cartoon.
b What hazards can you see?
c What happened?
d What caused it?
e How would you prevent it?
f What signs would you put where?

Trip-up Trev
a Name the items in the cartoon.
b What hazards can you see?
c What happened?
d What caused it?
e How would you prevent it?
f What signs would you put where?

Freefall Fred
a Name the items in the cartoon.
b What hazards can you see?
c What happened?
d What caused it?
e How would you prevent it?
f What signs would you put where?

Oily Oliver
a Name the items in the cartoon.
b What hazards can you see?
c What happened?
d What caused it?
e How would you prevent it?
f What signs would you put where?

Gauges: Too much pressure!

Objective: To extend vocabulary connected with different types of measurement and look at useful phrases for describing rising and falling quantities.

▶ **1 Look and write**

Look at the gauges and match each one with a name in the box. Write the correct names in the first column of the table.

> decibel counter   flow meter   measuring tank   pressure gauge
> thermometer   speedometer   scales   ammeter   clock/timer

Name	Measures	Sentence
1 scales	weight (kilogrammes)	d
2		
3		
4		
5		
6		
7		
8		
9		

▶ **2 Talk and write**

With a partner, discuss what each gauge measures. Write the measurement for each one in the second column of the table.

▶ **3 Read and choose**

Complete the third column of the table with the statement that matches the relevant gauge.

  a Don't allow liquid levels to shoot up above the 80 mark.

  b The volume should be maintained between 38 and 70.

  c Watch that it doesn't rise any higher than 80 degrees.

  d It's too light if it dips below 25.

  e The speed shouldn't fall below 25.

  f If it climbs to 80, there's too much pressure.

  g Don't let the flow drop to below 25.

  h Use your watch and keep within 40 and 70 minutes.

  i The power should remain between 40 and 70.

▶ **4 Sort the verbs**

Look at the statements in Task 3 again. Find other verbs to put in each column in the table on page 140.

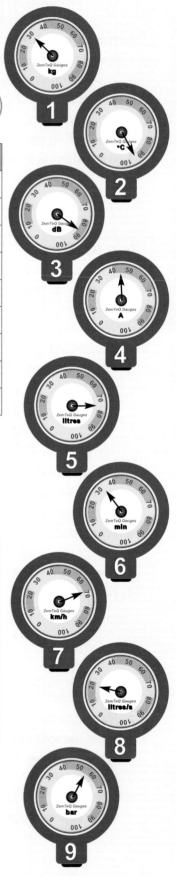

6 | Excavation

Objective: To review vocabulary connected with excavation and practise describing potential hazards connected with excavation.

▶ 1 Think and talk

Talk with a partner. Answer these questions about excavation.

1 What sort of machinery is used on an excavation site?
2 What are the risks and hazards of using machinery on site?
3 What are the other risks and hazards of working on an excavation site?

▶ 2 Read and write

Work with a partner. Read the clues and complete the crossword.

Across

3 Gloves will protect workers' hands when using machinery or a sharp _____.

4 Many hazardous machines are fitted with a _____ for protection.

6 There should be signs on site that tell people to _____ _____ from a potential hazard.

8 A _____ is a machine used to remove liquid.

13 If the support of a structure inadequate, it can _____.

14 Workers will need to _____ _____ support if there is danger of collapse.

16 A thorough _____ of the site must be conducted before work begins.

17 The health and safety inspector must _____ all machinery before it is used.

Down

1 On an excavation site, machinery is used to _____ holes.

2 Clearly _____ routes where the public can walk safely.

3 Rising water can _____ workers.

5 Excavation work can sometimes _____ buildings that are close to the site.

7 The public should not have _____ to a site when machinery is being used.

9 Workers will need to _____ _____ any structures that look unstable.

10 The company should _____ all workers with protective clothing on site.

11 When using drills, dust can make it difficult to _____.

12 Employers must not _____ workers to dangerous chemicals.

15 Workers should wear a _____ when using most machinery on site.

▶ 3 Discuss

Answer these questions in small groups.

1 Have you worked on an excavation or a large construction site?
2 What machinery did you use?
3 What potential hazards were you exposed to?

Objective: To become more familiar with useful vocabulary and phrases for discussing problems and solutions.

▶ **1** 🎧 **1:18 Listen and write**

Listen to the conversation between Jimmy and a shop assistant and write the missing words and phrases below.

SA Good morning. **1** _____?

J   Yes, I have a complaint. There is a **2** _____ with the TV I bought here last week. It's **3** _____.

SA **4** _____?

J   Well, firstly, it doesn't **5** _____ sometimes. And secondly, the plug **6** _____.

SA So ... what exactly do you want us to do with it, sir?

J   Well, you can **7** _____ it, give me **8** _____, or give me a new one.

SA I can **9** _____ it for you immediately, sir.

J   Thank you, but can you **10** _____ please? I have an **11** _____ to go to.

SA Certainly, if you can **12** _____, sir.

You are doing a job in the workshop and find that your new tool from stores is defective. You take it back and talk to the stores clerk about what you would like to happen. However, he has different ideas ...

You are the teacher. You have asked one of the students to fetch a TV, DVD-player and overhead projector for the class. You find that the equipment does not work. Talk to the student about the problems and try to find a solution to the problems. Keep your cool!

▶ **2** **Find and choose**

Write 1–12 next to the words and phrases that have a similar meaning to those from the conversation. Use some numbers more than once.

a not functioning _____
b get a move on _____
c start _____
d fix _____
e speed up _____
f do you need any assistance _____
g power up _____
h a refund _____
i overheats _____
j broken _____
k mend _____
l step on it _____
m fault _____
n what specifically is the problem _____
o exchange _____
p engagement _____
q hold on _____

Take a malfunctioning car back to the salesroom or garage from where you bought it. Explain what the problems are and what you want them to do about it. Remember to stay calm – don't lose your temper!

▶ **3** **Read and speak**

With a partner, act out the conversation several times using different words and phrases from Task 2.

Two workmates are out in the oilfield and their truck breaks down. They call their boss to talk about their problems and get some solutions.

▶ **4** **Read and write**

a Read the scenarios opposite and choose one.
b With a partner, write out the conversation using words and phrases from Tasks 1 and 2.
c Practise your conversation and then perform it for the class.

You are in the canteen with some friends and realize that your food is off. It tastes disgusting. Take the food back and talk to the cook.

Activate your vocabulary
Go to page 152.

Transport safety

1 | Transport safety

Objectives: To review and extend vocabulary for discussing transport safety. To practise listening for gist, and for specific words and information.

▶ 1 Walk and talk

a Discuss the questions below with a partner and answer as many as you can.

1 Where should pedestrians cross the road?
2 What should drivers do when they want to turn right?
3 You need to walk very near a crane. What do you do?
4 When can vehicles drive on pedestrian routes?
5 When is a site vehicle most likely to injure pedestrians?
6 What is the speed limit in your area?
7 Have you hit a stationary object when driving?
8 What colour are the walkways and stairwells where you work?
9 Where can you find anti-slip paint and banisters?
10 What accident black spots are there around your plant?
11 When working on top of a building, how can you stop yourself from falling off?
12 Is your company site well-lit?
13 Have you seen uneven floors and holes around the site?

b Walk around the class asking the questions to see if you can get any different answers.

▶ 2 ⓐ 1:19 Listen and answer

Listen to Richard's lecture on transport safety for pedestrians. What four types of hazard does he mention?

_____

_____

_____

_____

▶ 3 ⊚ 1:20 Listen and write

Listen to the lecture again and try to complete as many gaps in the transcript below as you can.

Hello, I hope you are all well today. This morning, we will look at **1** _____ safety, especially the safety of **2** _____, that is, people walking about. We looked at hazards in the last unit, so now we will think about how to prevent accidents.

First of all, avoiding **3** _____, trips and falls. Risk assessments are important and you – the workers – should be thinking about **4** _____ floors, badly lit stairways, puddles from leaking roofs and staying in the correct **5** _____. You must record all cleaning and maintenance work and make sure anti-slip covers are on stairs, **6** _____ and walkways. And remember ... use warning signs for washed floors.

Secondly, falls from height. Guard **7** _____ and barriers will prevent many falls, also fencing, toe boards and, sometimes, safety nets. Banisters or **8** _____ on stairways should always be used, and holes in floors filled or fenced. Key to preventing accidents is: using non-slip surfaces, **9** _____ and maintenance.

Thirdly, **10** _____ with moving vehicles injure many people in and out of work every year. It is important to separate pedestrians and vehicles and have clear walkways and clearly marked pedestrian crossings. Entrances, exits and blind corners to buildings are accident **11** _____, so the use of guard rails and barriers by workers is very important. Loading and unloading areas are also black spots and **12** _____ must be used.

Finally, preventing accidents caused by striking against fixed or **13** _____ objects. Simple. Use good lighting – yes, just turn it on. Use the walkways. Know what signs mean and ... how many times have I said it? ... Use your PPE.

▶ 4 Find the words

Look at the wordsearch. How many words and phrases can you find from the lecture in three minutes? Work in teams.

B	Y	S	L	I	P	S	T	R	I	P	S	A	N	D	F	A	L	L	S	H	V	J	L	S
N	E	F	E	N	C	I	N	G	J	T	R	A	N	S	P	O	R	T	X	G	N	P	G	P
U	S	S	O	A	O	Q	L	B	A	D	L	Y	L	I	T	V	C	J	W	K	E	E	C	E
C	T	B	S	I	G	N	S	V	T	O	E	B	O	A	R	D	S	Y	V	J	T	D	O	E
R	A	L	C	H	U	T	E	S	A	N	D	H	O	I	S	T	S	N	O	E	S	E	L	D
O	I	A	H	O	N	P	A	W	A	L	K	W	A	Y	H	X	I	L	Z	X	F	S	L	L
S	R	C	S	L	N	X	S	Y	U	N	E	V	E	N	F	L	O	O	R	I	E	T	I	I
S	W	K	D	E	S	T	A	T	I	O	N	A	R	Y	O	B	J	E	C	T	B	R	S	M
I	A	S	R	S	R	B	L	I	N	D	C	O	R	N	E	R	U	U	Y	H	M	I	I	I
N	Y	P	G	E	E	N	T	R	A	N	C	E	H	A	N	T	I	S	L	I	P	A	O	T
G	Y	O	Q	M	W	R	A	I	L	S	A	N	D	B	A	R	R	I	E	R	S	N	N	A
S	H	T	F	A	L	L	F	R	O	M	H	E	I	G	H	T	P	U	D	D	L	E	S	O

Objectives: To review vocabulary for hazards connected with transport and pedestrian safety. To practise writing short, clear e-mails in an appropriate style.

▶ 1   Complete the table

Think about the lecture on transport safety that you heard in Lesson 1 and complete the table. For some items, you will have to use your own ideas.

	Hazard type 1 Slips, trips and falls	**Hazard type 2** Falls from height	**Hazard type 3** Collisions with moving vehicles	**Hazard type 4** Striking stationary objects
Cause				
Prevention				
Injury as a result				

▶ 2   Talk about yourself

Have you had experiences involving accidents or near misses around the company site because of the hazards in the table? Tell another person about them or share them with the class.

▶ 3   Read and reply

a Read Jimmy's e-mail. What information does he need?

_____

_____

_____

b Write a reply. Include the following:
- Give information about some accidents that have happened in your section.
- Suggest ways that pedestrian safety can be improved.

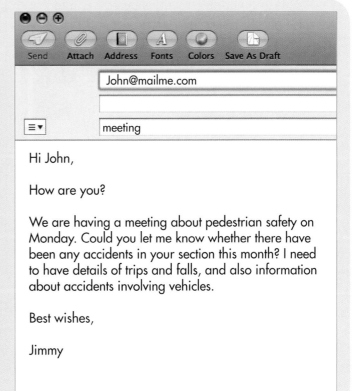

Send   Attach   Address   Fonts   Colors   Save As Draft

John@mailme.com

meeting

Hi John,

How are you?

We are having a meeting about pedestrian safety on Monday. Could you let me know whether there have been any accidents in your section this month? I need to have details of trips and falls, and also information about accidents involving vehicles.

Best wishes,

Jimmy

Objective: To use prepositions of direction and raise awareness of formal and informal language for asking for and giving directions.

▶ 1 Look and discuss

Complete the phrases using words from the box. Sometimes more than one answer is possible.

1 go around _____
2 go up/down _____
3 keep _____
4 take the _____
5 go straight _____
6 walk over _____
7 go under _____
8 turn _____
9 go through _____

> the bridge   second left/right
> the building   on   the steps
> left/right   the traffic island   the stairs
> the pedestrian bridge   going

▶ 2 Talk about the picture

Talk about the directions (a–l) shown in the picture using the phrases from Task 1. Test each other on directions by pointing to parts of the picture.

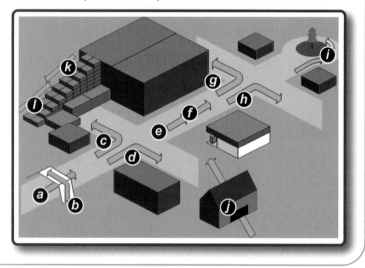

▶ 3 Write and tell

Write directions from a starting point (A) to a destination (B) in your plant or town. Then read them to the class. Tell them what the starting point is, but let them guess the destination.

▶ 4 Reorder and write

The questions below ask for directions to the toilet. Reorder them and decide whether they are formal or informal.

1 toilet know do the way you to the?
  _____
  _____

2 mate loo where's the hey?
  _____
  _____

3 to mate way bathroom the which?
  _____
  _____

4 you to to me can please the how tell restroom get?
  _____
  _____

5 from get WC how here you do the to?
  _____
  _____

6 lavatory is the nearest where please?
  _____
  _____

7 please mind directing do the me to you washroom?
  _____
  _____

▶ 5 A to B

As a class, complete the columns on page 143 with five more starting points (A) and five more destinations (B). Then move around the class asking directions from an A to B of your choice.

Objective: To review vocabulary for departments and places in a company and practise asking for and giving directions.

▶ 1 Departments in a company

Match the departments (a–j) with their definitions (1–10).

a	Accounts	____	**1**	does most of the day-to-day paperwork
b	Research & Development	____	**2**	main office
c	Administration	____	**3**	checks that standards of services and products are high
d	Quality Control	____	**4**	deals with money paid, received, borrowed or owed
e	Maintenance	____	**5**	deals with selling things
f	Payroll	____	**6**	produces brochures, reports and other information about the company
g	Human Resources	____	**7**	calculates salaries and payment
h	Communications	____	**8**	keeps machines working and fixes problems
i	Sales & Marketing	____	**9**	develops new products and looks at new ideas
j	Headquarters	____	**10**	manages and organizes staff

▶ 2 What's it called?

What are the names of the places below?

1 The welcome area that visitors report to. r_____
2 The main storage area for large items. w_____
3 The place where food and drink is served. c_____
4 The area(s) where supplies are kept. s_____
5 The place where reports and data are kept. r_____ o_____
6 A machine that reduces the size of rubbish. w_____ c_____
7 Rooms or building where there are chemicals. l_____
8 A building or area where products are manufactured. p_____

▶ 3 Look and check

With a partner, look at the map on the next page.

a Talk about what you can see, e.g., eating areas, car parks.
b Make sure you understand the vocabulary below the map.

▶ 4 Give directions

Work in groups of three. Student A should look at the map on the next page; Student B should look at the map on page 141 and Student C should look at the map on page 142. Make sure you start at the correct place, marked with an arrow. Take it in turns to ask directions to places on your map that are not labelled and then mark the location on the map with the correct number. Compare your maps at the end.

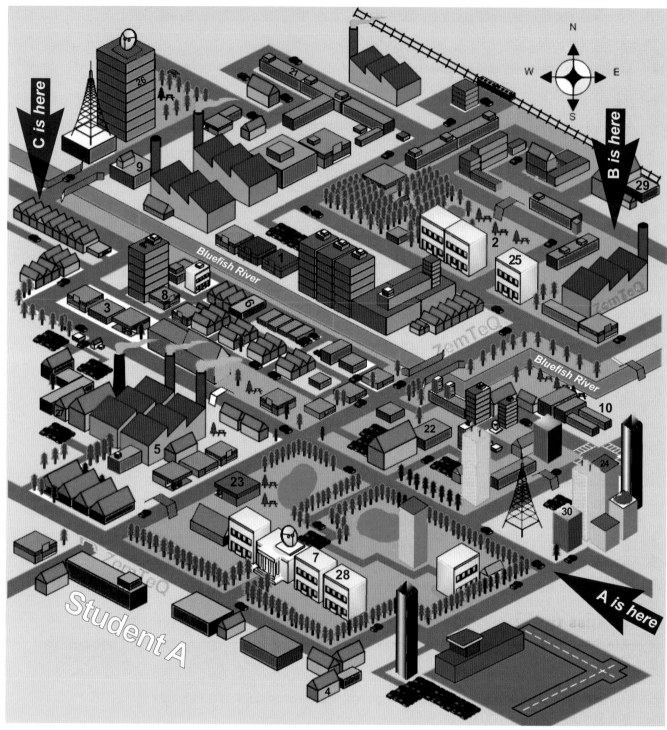

1 Executive Restaurant	**11** Training Centre	**21** Waste Compactor
2 Lunch Area 7	**12** Warehouse 91/b	**22** Maintenance
3 ZemTeQ Bank	**13** Stores	**23** Gas/Petrol Station 3
4 ZemTeQ Travel Agency	**14** Security Head Office	**24** Payroll
5 Plant 3	**15** Canteen 6	**25** R&D
6 Workshop 19	**16** Shower Block 11	**26** Records Office
7 Reception	**17** Administration	**27** Accounts
8 ZemTeQ Medical Centre	**18** HQ	**28** Sales & Marketing
9 Communications Centre	**19** Labs	**29** Pensions Office
10 Human Resources	**20** Quality Control	**30** H&S Headquarters

Objective: To practise using imperatives and language for rules and obligation to talk about road signs.

▶ 1 Look and match

Match the road signs A–L to their meanings (1–12).

1 don't veer or turn right ____
2 drop off cargo here ____
3 don't come in here ____
4 don't turn around ____
5 don't go faster than 15 miles per hour ____
6 you need permission ____
7 don't park here, ambulances and fire engines need access ____
8 drive at 20 miles per hour or under ____
9 no people allowed to walk in ____
10 don't leave your car outside this entrance ____
11 don't turn left or take the left route ____
12 no truck weighing more than seven and a half tonnes ____

▶ 2 Look and identify

Look at the road signs M–Y. With a partner, discuss what they mean and where you might see them.

▶ 3 Think and chat

With a partner, decide what sort of road signs you would see in the following places.

1 a narrow road
2 a loading bay outside a warehouse
3 a car park
4 a petrol station
5 a pedestrian area

▶ 4 Discuss the questions

a What sort of road signs can you see around the buildings and roads where you work?

b Would you remove any, or put up extra signs if you could? Why?

Objectives: To practise careful reading and listening in order to make decisions. To use language connected with forklift safety.

▶ 1 Look and label

Look at the picture of the forklift truck and label it using the words and phrases in the box.

> wheel ~~horn~~ roof guard battery steering wheel
> driver's seat tyres indicator forks mirror

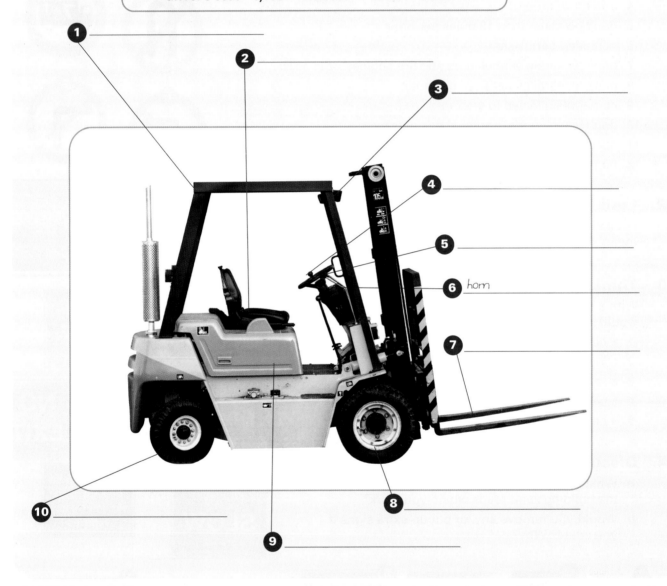

6 horn

▶ 2 Think and chat

With a partner, talk about the forklift.

a Discuss what each part does.

b Add more labels for other parts of the forklift that you can identify.

▶ 3 Read, listen and decide

Work in groups of three. Take it in turns to read out the situation in each step and decide what to do. You will need to refer back to the signs in Lesson 5. Find your way out of the maze by answering correctly.

Situation: Jimmy needs to deliver a load of pallets to Warehouse 2. He doesn't have a lot of experience with the forklift, but he is qualified. **Start at 8.**

1 Jimmy sees sign **N**. The supervisor checks Jimmy's docket and tells him to park here. **Go to 5**

2 He sees his mate and stops to chat. Looking up, he sees sign **G**.
  a He keeps talking as no one is around. **Go to 12**
  b He drives off with his friend, but forgets a crate and has to return to the bay. **Go to 32**

3 He arrives in Workshop 2 and reverses into a space. While reversing, he:
  a honks the horn. **Go to 42**
  b puts on the siren and lights and uses his mirror. **Go to 26**
  c shouts 'Move away!' **Go to 43**

4 He notices sign **E**.
  a He turns right. **Go to 12**
  b He veers left. **Go to 38**

5 He sees another sign – **O**, but the 'Super' told him to park at **N**.
  a He decides to do what the supervisor says and park. **Go to 40**
  b He offers the supervisor a cigarette. **Go to 41**

6 He sees sign **A** saying not to drive less than 20, so he speeds up. **Go to 14**

7 He parks and sees sign **I** above. What now?
  a He decides it will be OK for five minutes and goes to look for the supervisor. **Go to 22**
  b He moves the vehicle, as it is forbidden to park here. **Go to 13**

8 He picks up the forklift and goes to loading, where he sees sign **Y**.
  a He powers down the motor and uses a torch to find the load. **Go to 36**
  b He turns off the motor and finds a foreman to ask. **Go to 17**
  c He leaves the forklift running and looks for the load. **Go to 31**

9 He notices sign **R**, stops and looks both ways. **Go to 12**

10 He observes sign **P** and notices that there are a lot of pedestrians about.
  a He cuts across the walkway to save time. **Go to 6**
  b He slows down, takes care and uses his horn. **Go to 24**

11 He notices sign **V** near the gate and:
  a goes the opposite way. **Go to 12**
  b goes the way the sign suggests. **Go to 30**

12 The supervisor arrives shouting that Jimmy will never drive at ZemTeQ again. Think why and start again. **Go to 8**

13 He drives around loading and stops when he sees sign **K**. What now?
  a He turns around and goes back. **Go to 36**
  b He calls the supervisor. **Go to 1**
  c He carries on. There's no one around to see. **Go to 19**

14 He glances at sign **T**. There's a problem.

a He changes his mind, slows down and turns back. **Go to 20**
  b There's nothing about, so he speeds up. **Go to 42**

15 He thinks he is on the wrong route. Then he notices sign **C**.
  a He keeps going. **Go to 27**
  b He turns back for help. **Go to 34**

16 Later he sees sign **X**. It is quite high, so he takes off his hat and goggles to read it. **Go to 12**

17 He tells him to park under sign **U**.
  a He goes to the pallet with *Jimmy* written on it and thinks it must be his. **Go to 32**
  b He looks for the loading manager to ask him for instructions. **Go to 35**
  c He goes to the inquiry office. **Go to 33**

18 That's better. He sees a short cut left but then notices sign **F**.
  a He decides to keep right, even though he'll be late. **Go to 2**
  b No one is watching, so he takes the short cut. **Go to 37**

19 This is bad, he cannot drive forward or back. The supervisor arrives looking angry. **Go to 12**

20 Jimmy is in the warehouse area with a low battery. He sees sign **X**.
  a He parks up, takes out a cigarette and asks for a light. **Go to 9**
  b He puts on his seat belt and carries on. **Go to 23**
  c He puts on his hat and goggles, then turns on his lights because of the dark. **Go to 10**
  d He looks for somewhere to charge his battery. **Go to 6**

21 He sees sign **K**. He doesn't want to be late, so he enters. **Go to 12**

22 Nobody is there, so he returns to the forklift and parks out of the bay. He sees sign **J**. The supervisor tells him to move. **Go to 28**

23 He sees sign **Q**. He stops and waits for traffic coming the other way to pass. **Go to 29**

24 His mobile rings. He stops and sees sign **Y**.
  a He answers it, as it might be an emergency. **Go to 12**
  b He stops his engine and turns off his mobile. **Go to 3**
  c He cancels the call and carries on. **Go to 11**

25 He sees sign **T** and goes into the same area as other forklifts. He uses the horn to clear the others, as he has priority. **Go to 34**

26 You have helped Jimmy out of the maze. He made a few mistakes, but is becoming a good forklift driver. Well done.

27 Sign **D** is on the wall nearby. Jimmy then sees a large lorry enter.
  a He decides to ignore it. **Go to 39**
  b He decides to chase after it at high speed. **Go to 42**

28 He drives on, going around several corners.

His tyres feel a little flat. Then he sees sign **L**, so he checks his permit. **Go to 1**

29 Nothing comes. He looks back and sees sign **S**. He realizes he has made some mistakes. **Go to 9**

30 He looks up at sign **W**, but is not sure of the height of the forklift.
  a He decides to carry on, as it should be OK. **Go to 12**
  b He drives out of the area. **Go to 16**

31 He's racing at 25 mph. Then he sees sign **B**.
  a He slows down. 'Be safe, not sorry'. **Go to 4**
  b He carries on at the same speed, as there are no vehicles or pedestrians about. **Go to 21**

32 He loads and drives off. As he speeds up, he sees sign **B**.
  a He keeps going at 20 mph as there is nobody there. **Go to 37**
  b He slows down, as he knows speed limits are vital. **Go to 18**

33 As he arrives, he sees a huge truck reversing by sign **D**.
  a He does nothing, and lets the truck continue. **Go to 41**
  b He whistles and tells the driver he can't drive there. **Go to 4**

34 He sees a place to stop. Then he sees sign **J**, but parks anyway. **Go to 12**

35 The manager helps Jimmy load. After driving off, he realizes he has forgotten one of the boxes. He sees sign **C**.
  a He doesn't go back for the box, as he can get it next time. **Go to 20**
  b He turns back to get the box. **Go to 14**

36 He sees he is parked near sign **H**.
  a He moves on to another place. **Go to 7**
  b He decides to load up here. **Go to 39**

37 He needs to go right, but sees sign **E**. He isn't sure what to do, so he:
  a stops and smokes a cigarette. **Go to 7**
  b drives around to find another way. **Go to 2**

38 He sees sign **W** and doesn't know if his forklift is too high.
  a He goes the long route. **Go to 15**
  b He stops and calls the supervisor to check. **Go to 34**
  c He thinks he should be OK. **Go to 25**

39 The supervisor arrives shouting: 'Get out!' and, 'You will never drive at ZemTeQ again.' Think why and start again. **Go to 8**

40 There's a clear sign saying not to do this. The supervisor is furious. He gives Jimmy a warning and tells him to start the job again. **Go to 8**

41 Bang! The truck hits the building and it is Jimmy's fault. Start again. **Go to 8**

42 Smash! He hits another forklift. Think why this happens and start again. **Go to 8**

43 Smack! He hits a pedestrian, but he isn't seriously hurt. He gets a final warning. Start again. **Go to 8**

Objective: To become more familiar with useful vocabulary and phrases for making small talk about recent events.

People commonly make small talk about recent events and news about their company.

▶ **1** 🎧 **1:21 Listen and write**

Listen to the conversation and write the missing words and phrases below.

J Good morning, Richard. Have you heard **1** _____?

R Good morning. No, what's happened?

J Well, the new furnace in Plant 3 has **2** _____.

R When did it **3** _____?

J It blew up **4** _____ ten last night.

R Was anyone **5** _____?

J Yeah. Three **6** _____ went to hospital with serious burns.

R What **7** _____ the incident?

J Well, it's only **8** _____, but people say the engineer **9** _____ on shift. He's such a lazy man.

R Jimmy, you shouldn't believe gossip. Let's wait for the incident report. **10** _____, have you heard about the new manager in stores? He ...

▶ **2** **Find and choose**

Write 1–10 next to the words and phrases that have a similar meaning to those from the conversation. Use some numbers more than once.

a	hurt	____	**m**	lead to	____
b	brought about	____	**n**	wounded	____
c	the announcement	____	**o**	dropped off	____
d	men	____	**p**	something like	____
e	around	____	**q**	the hearsay	____
f	although	____	**r**	the headlines	____
g	occur	____	**s**	but	____
h	chaps	____	**t**	blokes	____
i	harmed	____	**u**	exploded	____
j	a rumour	____	**v**	nodded off	____
k	roughly at	____	**w**	take place	____
l	gave rise to	____			

▶ **3** **Read and speak**

With a partner, act out the conversation several times using different words and phrases from Task 2.

▶ **4** **Read and write**

a Read the scenarios opposite and choose one.
b With a partner, write out the conversation using words and phrases from Tasks 1 and 2.
c Practise your conversation and then perform it for the class.

A couple of work buddies are sitting in the canteen talking about all the gossip they have heard over the last week or so. One of them has heard some very interesting things about the line manager.

Two friends are just clocking in and start chatting as they are a little early. They talk about last night's TV and especially the news from around the country and world. They try to explain to each other what they remember about the big stories.

Two co-workers are in the tea room talking about an accident one of them saw in the workshop earlier that week. The other worker is very curious and asks lots of questions to find out more.

A chap at work has missed a health and safety meeting that was very important. A friend tries to fill him in on exactly what took place so he can catch up.

The teacher and a student are chatting before the class starts. Both have funny stories about things that happened to them since the last class.

Activate your vocabulary
Go to page 152.

Working at height

1 | Working at height

Objective: To focus on general terms for discussing working at height.

▶ 1 Look and talk
a Discuss what you can see in the pictures.
b Can you think of any other types of height equipment?

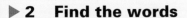

▶ 2 Find the words
Try to find 19 words connected with working at height in the wordsearch.

▶ 3 Walk and talk
a Discuss the questions below with a partner, and answer as many as you can.

1. Have you fallen? When? Where? Why?
2. How many injuries due to falls from height happened last year in your company?
3. Do you suffer from vertigo or have 'a bad head for heights'?
4. What sort of height equipment is used in your company?
5. Would you like to try parachuting?
6. What is the highest point on your company's site?
7. Do you have any fragile roofs at work?
8. What do you use ladders and stepladders for?

b Walk around the class, asking and answering the questions with as many people as possible.

C	S	L	V	D	N	U	S
O	A	S	W	J	Y	N	E
I	S	Q	Q	X	K	P	C
Z	C	G	O	O	P	R	U
V	E	R	T	I	G	O	R
F	N	T	V	J	C	T	E
Y	D	E	H	O	H	E	T
S	P	R	P	I	E	C	O
C	A	G	O	N	R	T	W
A	R	A	I	J	R	E	E
F	A	S	N	U	Y	D	R
F	C	T	T	R	P	T	P
O	H	E	S	I	I	A	L
L	U	P	O	E	C	N	A
D	T	L	F	S	K	G	T
F	I	A	C	O	E	L	F
R	N	D	O	A	R	E	O
A	G	D	N	K	T	K	R
G	F	E	T	F	R	F	M
I	I	R	A	A	E	C	X
L	M	U	C	L	S	L	H
E	A	W	T	L	T	I	E
R	S	D	J	E	L	M	I
O	I	W	D	N	E	B	G
O	G	I	F	E	C	E	H
F	N	X	R	M	R	D	T

▶ 4 Look
The signs below are all connected with working at height. What do they mean?

Objective: To focus on terms for equipment used for working at height.

▶ 1 Find and match

Match the names of the equipment with the correct picture.

1 scaffold
2 cherry picker
3 access cradle
4 trestle
5 ladder
6 harness
7 stepladder

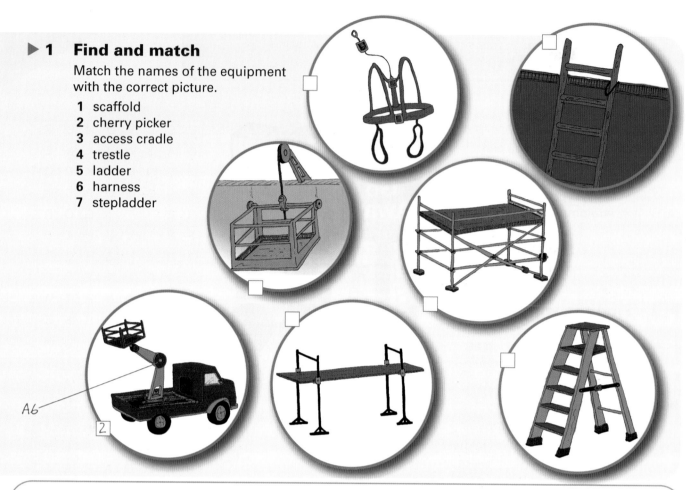

▶ 2 Match and label

Label the key parts in each picture using words and phrases from the table on page 143. Choose one part from each column to label each picture (five labels per picture).

▶ 3 Equipment quiz

Talk about the questions with a partner and answer as many as you can.

1 How many people should ascend a ladder at one time?
2 What should the angle of the ladder be?
3 How do you secure a ladder?
4 What is a cherry picker used for?
5 How many points of contact do you need when climbing a ladder?
6 What do you use a trestle for?
7 Which jobs should scaffolds and towers be used for?

▶ 4 Make it safe

With a partner, look at the signs opposite and decide which should be used with the equipment above.

3 | Ladder lecture

Objective: To practise listening for gist and specific information about ladder safety.

▶ 1 ⊙ 1:22 Listen and answer

Listen to the first part of Richard's lecture on ladder safety and note down your answers to the three questions below.

1 What is the number one cause of accidents with ladders at ZemTeQ?

_____

2 What are the two normal types of ladders?

_____

3 What are some problems linked with these two types of ladder?

▶ 2 ⊙ 1:23 Listen and write

Listen to the second part of the lecture and complete the ZemTeQ Ladder Safety Advice.

Remember, when you use a ladder:

1 Ask yourself or your **1** _____: is the ladder the best access to the job?
2 Check the **2** _____. The supporting wall and ground should be dry.
3 Make sure it is **3** _____. The inclination should be 1–4 or about 75 degrees.
4 Tie the **4** _____ to a strong support.
5 Check **5** _____ conditions. Wind and heavy rain are dangerous.
6 Have at least 1 metre of ladder above the **6** _____ point.
7 Avoid **7** _____.
8 Place paints and tools in a **8** _____ place.
9 Climb by using **9** _____ hands.
10 Wear **10** _____ footwear.
11 Clean and dry all dirty **11** _____.
12 Inspect ladder for **12** _____.
13 Maintain ladder **13** _____.
14 Transport **14** _____, ladders damage easily.
15 Store it in a **15** _____ place.

▶ 3 Look and match

a Look at the pictures and decide which are correct and incorrect.

b Match the correct pictures with the advice above.

Objectives: To practise describing situations and equipment in detail.
Further practice of vocabulary for ladder safety.

▶ 1 Unscramble and label

With a partner, unscramble the words.
Then use them to label the picture.

1 dwscnaih _____
2 ekbctu _____
3 ungr _____
4 wiondw _____
5 aleestddpr _____
6 rbdi _____
7 olrof _____
8 eroatofw _____
9 derdla _____
10 irgp _____
11 iet-dor _____
12 setli _____
13 senpgo _____
14 rahdaht _____
15 brebur oitfgon _____
16 tesp _____

▶ 2 Find ten differences

With a partner, sit back-to-back. Student A:
look at the picture above. Student B: look at
the picture on page 143. Find ten differences
and circle them on your picture.

▶ 3 Solve the crossword

Use the ladder rules from Lesson 3 to solve
the crossword.

¹F ²R O N T   ³W   ⁴D
    ⁵W
⁶S   ⁷S   ⁸T   ⁹L
    ¹⁰T   ¹¹R
¹²P   ¹³U
¹⁴S   ¹⁵S

Across
1 Always face the job and work f_____ on.
3 Never climb a ladder in wet or w_____ weather.
6 Look for missing nails or s_____.
8 Never leave t_____ on ladder.
10 Never use short-term or t_____ repairs.
12 Never place ladder in p_____ of water.
13 Make sure the ladder feet aren't on u_____ ground.
14 Check for oil-s_____ on rungs.
15 Stepladders need non-s_____ footing.

Down
2 Never stretch or overr_____ on a ladder.
4 Clean all d_____ rungs before use.
5 Check for w_____-rot before using.
7 S_____ should have no cracks or warping.
9 L_____ ladder at 75 degrees.
11 Check for splits on r_____.

5 | How high? How tall? How wide?

Objective: To practise asking and answering questions using language for different units of quantity.

▶ 1 Look and match

a Match the words (1–13) with the pictures (a–m).
b Test each other on the new words by pointing at the pictures and saying the correct words.

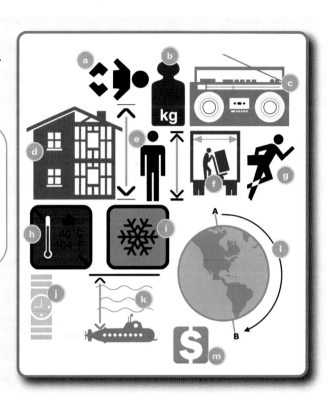

a

1 heavy	___		**8** fast	___
2 tall	___		**9** wide	___
3 much	___		**10** far	___
4 long	___		**11** cold	___
5 high	___		**12** hot	___
6 loud	___		**13** deep	___
7 old	___			

▶ 2 Complete the questions and answers

a Complete the questions below using words from box a (Task 1).
b Choose a number from box b and a unit of measurement from box c for each question.

b

8	148
4	15
30	15
2½	3
180	80–90
28	255
27	

Question	Unit	Measurement	Your company
1 How ___long___ is a normal shift?	8	hrs	
2 How _____ is the main entrance gate?			
3 How _____ is the water tower?			
4 How _____ is the big boss?			
5 How _____ is the local pool?			
6 How _____ is it outside at noon?			
7 How _____ is the canteen chiller?			
8 How _____ is the nearest restaurant?			
9 How _____ can the plant noise normally get?			
10 How _____ is each pair of goggles?			
11 How _____ can a forklift go?			
12 How _____ is the maximum pallet load?			
13 How _____ is the company?			

c

hrs	m
m	km
°C	ft
dB	mph
°C	years
cm	kg
euros	

▶ 3 Write and compare

Write the answers for your company. Compare your answers with others in the class.

▶ 4 Ask the class

Write questions using the prompts on page 143 to ask other students about their homes or work sections. Ask and note the answers of five students. Then give a short report to the class.

Objectives: To raise awareness of different written communications in health and safety contexts. To practise editing written text and responding to written requests.

Jimmy has received a lot of messages about jobs that involve working at height. He has them on his office bulletin board so he can read them easily and decide if there will be any problems in issuing permits to work.

▶ 1 Skim the board

a Look at the messages quickly and decide which ones are:

1 e-mails
2 notes from other people
3 telephone messages
4 reminders to self
5 letters

b What are the main characteristics of each?

g
Hey, have to repair radio mast. Need a lot of heavy tools up ladder. O.K, I guess. Thanks
Tim

b
To: Jimmy
From: Sid
Date: 27/6   Time: 9:50
Need to clear bird nests in Water Tower 2. Will use cherry picker. No harness necessary. Not much room for equipment in cage.
taken by: Derek

h
Hey Jimmy!
Will get up in cherry picker to check new roofing on Workshop 2. Some power lines nearby. No problem. Simon

k
Jim,
Must clean racking in Warehouse 6. Will climb with care. Tom Smith

e
Date: 26/6
To: Jimmy   From: Greg
Stepladder's a little short. Should be OK on top step. Maybe I can work with Dennis on same ladder as space is small.

c
Some scaffold poles rusty for canteen job!!

a
James
Need to clean windows Warehouse 3. Each window 2x3m. Ground a little muddy. OK I think.
Toby

d
Heavy equipment needed for access cradle for Tower 4!!

f
To: Jimmy
From: Steve
Date: 27/6   Time: 9:45
Will ascend in access cradle to clean Water Tower 4. Not checked by maintenance. Looks OK. Pls call back
taken by: Derek

o
Need trestle to paint toilet 4. Some water on floors. Will wear sandals for safety. Henry

j
To: Jimmy@ZemTeQ.com
From: Sam
Subject: Permit to work
Will clean mezzanine in main warehouse. No guard rail! I will be very careful.
Thanks
Derek

l
To: Jimmy
From: Harry
Date: 27/6   Time: 9:56
Harness looks old and faded. But OK for easy job: roof guard rail inspection.
taken by: Derek (again!)

Dear Jimmy,
This regards the scaffold needed for the west wall of the old canteen. Mike will help me but he has no experience. I will tell him what to do. We have no toe boards, but I do not think it will be a problem.

Sincerely
Lenny Smith

i
Hello Jimmy
Want to use trestles to ele cleaning job near main gate. Have narrow boards but am experienced. Bill

n
Date: 29/6
To: Jimmy   From: Cam
Must check roofing. Will use harness on roof. Work will take a long time I think.

▶ 2 Who said what?

Write the names of the workers who told Jimmy the following:

1 access cradle not inspected _____
2 electricity cables near job _____
3 very little room to work _____
4 assistant not trained _____
5 straps are damaged _____
6 spills/leaks around job _____
7 shelving is dirty _____
8 no wide planking available _____
9 need more than one ladder _____

▶ 3   Correct and add

Below are a few of the important rules for the safe use of each piece of equipment at ZemTeQ. Jimmy has misspelt some of them, and left some out.

a Look through the safety rules and circle ten spelling errors.

Stepladder		Trestle		Scaffold	
1	Use correct sise for job	1	Must use wide boards	1	Equipment must be defect-free
2	No overreaching	2	Use on flat/dry base	2	Only trained personal
3	1 person aloud on ladder	3	Use corect PPE	3	Tow boards must be used

Ladder		Access cradle		Harness		Cherry picker	
1	Do not use on wet/uneven base	1	No obstruction on platform	1	Only use for short time	1	Attatch harness to cage
2	No heavy equipment/tools	2	Unspect before using	2	Must be guard rale at edge	2	Stay away from cables
3	Check for damige before job	3	Do not overload	3	Check for damage	3	Do not over-full

b Can you think of three or four extra rules?

▶ 4   Decide and write

a Read the messages and the rules again. In groups, decide if each job (a–o) should have a permit to work or not.

b Write notes or e-mails in response to the requests, confirming or refusing the permit. If the permit is refused, explain why and say what the worker must do to obtain one.

Example:

> To: Greg
> From: Jimmy
> Date: 27/6
>
> Sorry, can't issue a permit. You need to use two longer ladders because, according to the rules, you mustn't overreach on stepladders. Remember that only one person is allowed per ladder.

Objective: To become more familiar with useful vocabulary and phrases for starting conversations.

Learning how to start conversations can make work a better place.

▶ **1** 🎧 **1:24 Listen and write**

Listen and write the missing words and phrases below.

Did you see that 1 _____ last night?

2 _____, don't I know you?

Is this 3 _____?

Haven't seen you for 4 _____.

5 _____ day, isn't it?

See the 6 _____ last night, Dave?

Got a 7 _____, mate?

Hello, could you 8 _____?

Have you finished 9 _____ that?

Can I 10 _____ a few euros?

Have you heard 11 _____ about ...?

What are you 12 _____?

13 _____ this weekend?

Fancy 14 _____ later?

15 _____?

Two complete strangers start a conversation at dinn and find that they ha a lot of things in common, including working for the sam company.

You are a little nervous because yo are in an office waiti room, hanging arou for your interview fo a promotion. There are some people in the room you don't recognize and so yo try to start a conversa with them.

▶ **2** **Find and choose**

Write 1–14 next to the words and phrases that have a similar meaning to those from Task 1. Use some numbers more than once.

a looking at _____

b coming to my house _____

c a long time _____

d Have you heard _____

e cadge _____

f show _____

g help me out _____

h great _____

i What are you doing _____

j the joke _____

k free _____

l doing _____

m match _____

n occupied _____

▶ **3** **Choose and speak**

Match the replies (16–27) with some of the conversation starters (1–15) from Task 1.

16 With Jim Carrey? Very exciting. _____

17 Yep. Here you are. _____

18 Must be two or three years now. _____

19 Sure. How much do you need? _____

20 Can't. Got stuff on. _____

21 Yeah. But there's rain tomorrow. _____

22 I've heard it before. _____

23 Not sure. I'm Bill. _____

24 Nothing much. Fancy a tea? _____

25 Tell me. Quickly. _____

26 How did it finish? Nil nil? _____

27 No. It's all yours. _____

It's the first day for two new workers. They meet in the waiting room in the Admin block and start chatting.

You have some foreign visitors in your compa You see one in the canteen and go up to h and start a conversatio

There is a new stude in the class. It is you job to make her feel welcome and so you break the ice in the tea break.

▶ **4** **Read and write**

a Read the situations opposite and choose one.

b With a partner, write a conversation using words and phrases from Tasks 1 and 2.

c Practise your conversation and then perform it for the class.

Activate your vocabulary

Go to page 152.

Workplace manual handling

1 | Handling lecture

Objective: To focus on key terms for discussing handling, and to listen to dos and don'ts for handling procedures.

▶ **1   Look and label**

a Discuss what you can see in the picture.
b Look at the words in the box. Label the pictures a–o.

a sweat	**e** pallet mover	**i** watch	**m** backpack
b twist	**f** overweight	**j** thermometer	**n** crutch
c top shelf	**g** switch	**k** knees	**o** spill
d sack truck	**h** clock	**l** sharp	

▶ 2 Read and discuss

a With a partner, read the statements below and decide if they are true (T) or false (F).

1 40% of workers get a back injury at some time. ___ ___ ___
2 Injuries include sprains, cuts and amputations. ___ ___ ___
3 There are fewer injuries if someone is old and in cold temperatures. ___ ___ ___
4 Bending and stooping can cause injuries. ___ ___ ___
5 Body stress is higher for pulling than pushing. ___ ___ ___
6 Keep loads away from the body, with a soft grip. ___ ___ ___
7 Overweight people have fewer handling injuries. ___ ___ ___
8 Never carry loads in strong winds. ___ ___ ___
9 Avoid lifting very heavy or sharp items. ___ ___ ___

b Match each statement to the correct speech bubble in the picture on page 69.

▶ 3 ⓐ 2:1 Listen and correct

Listen to Richard's lecture about manual handling.

a Mark the statements from Task 2 as correct (✓) or incorrect (✗).
b In your notebook, rewrite the incorrect statements so that they are correct.

▶ 4 ⓐ 2:2 Solve the puzzle

Look at the clues and complete the crossword using key words from the lecture. Then listen to the lecture again to check your answers.

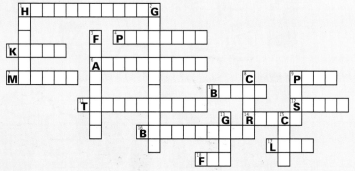

Across

1 general organization of work area
4 think about your foot _____
5 bend your _____
6 when an arm or leg is removed
7 handling without a machine
9 to drag backward
10 a rest
11 do this to see (three words)
12 bend over
14 to stretch for something
16 common handling injury (two words)
17 to raise something
18 overweight

Down

1 internal lifting injury
2 do this close to body when holding (three words)
3 to break or crack a bone
8 to bring an item in your hands
9 to force forward
13 strong wind
15 tuck it in

▶ 5 Write and speak

a Complete the sentences below about yourself.
b Read your sentences to your partner and discuss the similarities and differences.

1 Items I normally handle are _____.
2 The heaviest thing I lift is _____.
3 I normally take breaks at _____.
4 The most dangerous item I ever handled was _____.
5 My workmate _____ injured his _____ because _____.
6 I use _____ equipment to move _____.

2 | Sack truck instructions

Objective: To become more familiar with instruction language in a user guide or manual, and to write instructions in English.

▶ 1 Label and check

a Label the parts of the sack truck using the words and phrases from the box.

b Compare your answers in groups.

> width locking bar wheel height handlebar
> footplate hand grip depth footplate width

Safety Instructions
Sack truck: ZemTeQ *315*

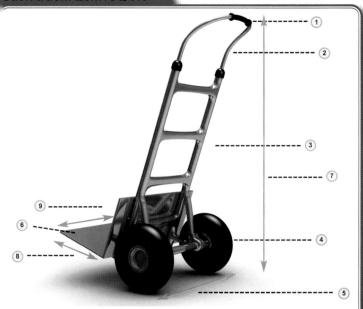

Safety instructions
Always load evenly with load centre of gravity near centre of **1** _____.
Get help with heavy load to avoid **2** _____.
Get assistance with wide loads to avoid overturning.
Never **3** _____ the truck.
Do not leave unattended when loaded.
Do not use on **4** _____ floor.
Use a **5** _____ to get up kerbs or steps.
Check for **6** _____ before use, especially the wheels.
Do not use if damaged.

Specifications
Max. load: 90 kg
7 _____: 1,100 mm
8 _____: 385 mm
Footplate width: **9** _____
Footplate depth: **10** _____
Wheel **11** _____: 155 mm

Use of truck
12 _____ footplate to accept load.
Undo **13** _____ on handlebar.
14 _____ handlebar to correct height.
Lock handlebar.
After use, close handle and fold up footplate.
15 _____ in safe, dry place.

▶ 2 Complete the text

Match the missing words (a–o) to the gaps in the safety instructions (1–15).

a	footplate	**i**	fold down
b	390 mm	**j**	overload
c	extend	**k**	lock
d	store	**l**	defects
e	uneven	**m**	width
f	ramp	**n**	250 mm
g	tipping	**o**	diameter
h	height		

▶ 3 Questions and answers

Here are ten answers to questions about the safety instructions. Write out the questions in your notebook.

1 So it's not too heavy to move.
2 Because the tyres puncture easily.
3 To help the truck onto the kerb.
4 Before you use it.
5 In a secure place that is not wet.
6 Fold up the footplate.
7 385 mm.
8 250 mm.
9 To accept the load.
10 Ask somebody to help.

▶ 4 Do-it-yourself

Now it's your turn. Prepare some instructions for a piece of equipment you know.

a Make a labelled diagram with safety instructions, specifications and how-to-use instructions.

b Explain your safety instructions to other people in the class.

c Check that others in the group have understood your instructions by asking three or four questions about the equipment.

Good lift technique

Getting your lifting technique right is very important in manual handling to avoid injury. Throughout the working day we lift items frequently; even a teacher needs to get it right.

▶ **1 Look and choose**

Manual lift instructions usually involve six stages:

1 Plan the lift
2 Get your feet right
3 Get a good grip
4 Lift smoothly
5 Move smoothly
6 Put down load

Choose the six photos which best match each of the stages.

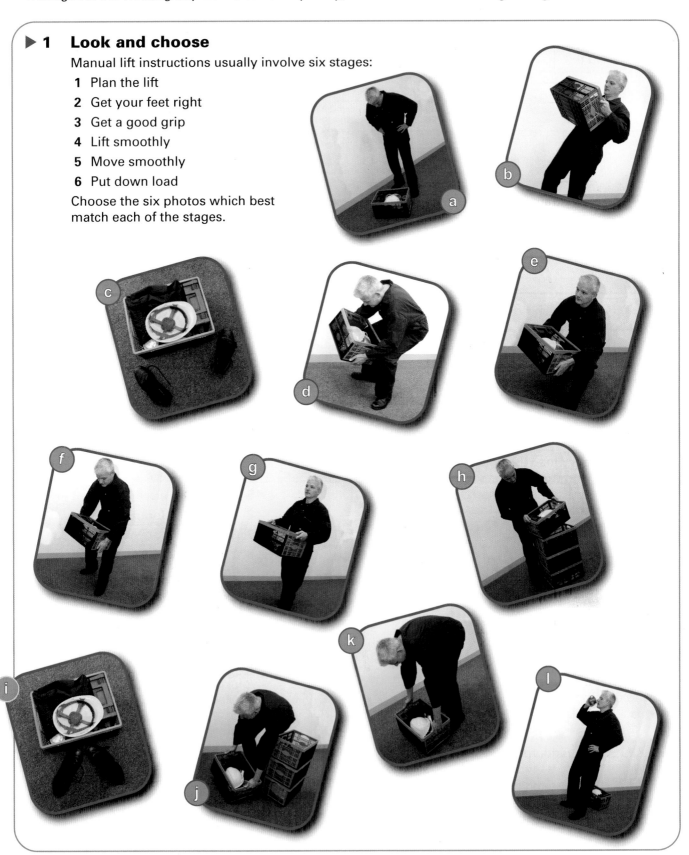

▶ 2 Give instructions

a With a partner, instruct each other how to lift a chair. Student A instructs, Student B lifts. Manual lifting instructions usually involve six stages. Can you think of six stages when lifting a chair?

1 _____
2 _____
3 _____
4 _____
5 _____
6 _____

b Demonstrate with your partner in front of the class. One person should instruct and one should lift.

▶ 3 Read and order

Put these stages of lifting technique in order.

a Raise the load to knee level and then to waist level, but do not bend your back more. _____

b As you start to lift, make sure the load is close to the body. The back and knees should be slightly bent to get a good hold. _____

c Then, check the route is clear and go forward without twisting. _____

d Finally, set the load down carefully and then slide it into position. _____

e Ask yourself: Can I use an aid? Do I need help? Where will I place it? _____

f Before lifting, stand with feet apart and then move one leg a little forward to give good balance. _____

▶ 4 Find the words

Complete the table below with words that have a similar meaning. Use words from the instructions in Task 3 and any others you can think of.

Pick up	Transport	Drop off

Objective: To practise transferring information onto a risk assessment form.

▶ 1 Find and match

Find similar words to a–h in the form below.

a surroundings _____

b large _____

c damaging _____

d results _____

e not enough _____

f not right _____

g education _____

h preparation _____

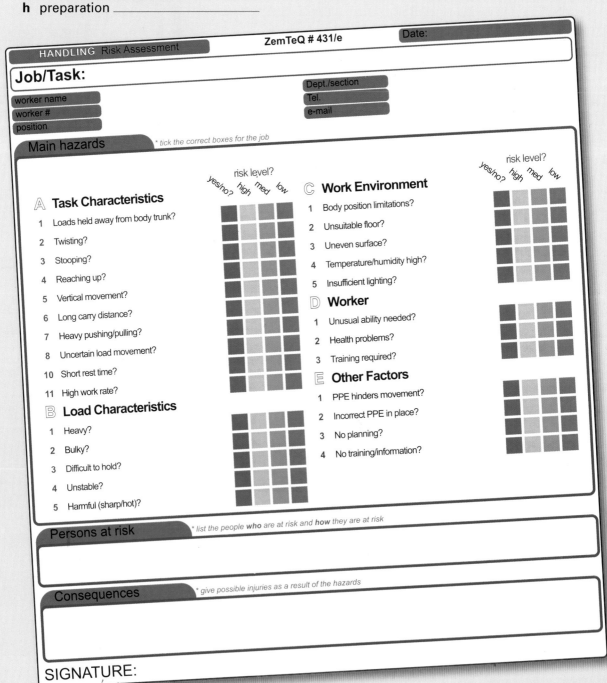

HANDLING Risk Assessment   ZemTeQ # 431/e   Date:

Job/Task:

worker name   Dept./section
worker #   Tel.
position   e-mail

Main hazards   * tick the correct boxes for the job

risk level? yes/no? high med low

A Task Characteristics

1 Loads held away from body trunk?
2 Twisting?
3 Stooping?
4 Reaching up?
5 Vertical movement?
6 Long carry distance?
7 Heavy pushing/pulling?
8 Uncertain load movement?
10 Short rest time?
11 High work rate?

B Load Characteristics

1 Heavy?
2 Bulky?
3 Difficult to hold?
4 Unstable?
5 Harmful (sharp/hot)?

C Work Environment

1 Body position limitations?
2 Unsuitable floor?
3 Uneven surface?
4 Temperature/humidity high?
5 Insufficient lighting?

D Worker

1 Unusual ability needed?
2 Health problems?
3 Training required?

E Other Factors

1 PPE hinders movement?
2 Incorrect PPE in place?
3 No planning?
4 No training/information?

Persons at risk   * list the people **who** are at risk and **how** they are at risk

Consequences   * give possible injuries as a result of the hazards

SIGNATURE:

▶ 2 Reorder and write

Jimmy phones Cam, a manager, about a handling job that involves moving hazardous chemicals. Cam asks him some questions in order to fill in a risk assessment form. Reorder the words in 1–7 to make Cam's questions and write each one above the correct answer (a–g). Then use the information in the conversation to complete the form opposite.

1 Jimmy what job is the?

2 details can give you me your?

3 the what characteristics are task?

4 the what load about?

5 area the how work is?

6 about what you?

7 else anything involved?

a _____

I need to move three hazardous chemical drums from the fertilizer plant to the petrochemical plant next door.

b _____

Well, there's medium risk for twisting and stooping. The same for heavy pulling, plenty of time for rest though.

c _____

I'm OK. No health problems and I'm fully trained. It's a standard job.

d _____

It's a heavy load with low risk and bulk. There's a high harm risk because of the chemicals. But I'll use full PPE, Cam.

e _____

Sure. Jimmy Jackson, number 4210 on extension 4961. I'm a health and safety department junior inspector. I'm at jimmyj@ZemTeQ.com.

f _____

The floors, lighting and temperature are fine. I've double-checked all of them.

g _____

Not really. All the PPE is here and I can move OK. I've planned it well, as I have all the job information here.

▶ 3 Write and present

Go to page 144. With a partner, choose one job request from Jimmy's noticeboard below and fill out a handling risk assessment form for it.

a Acetylene cylinders must be moved to furnace area

c Transfer new glass panes 15 x 45 kg to site office 14 ASAP. 2 men only.

Fetch hot water dispensers full and heated to sports field for half-time refreshments

m Need to shift loose wire cable now. Urgent – in warehouse 4 – no breaks until it is finished. It is very thick and sharp.

f Transport scaffold poles to new site in area 14 by 4 p.m. today. I know it is raining, but urgent.

g Load 30 x 10 kg boxes of nails onto pallets. I man job. Outside midday.

d Deliver ice bags 50 x 20 kg to canteen because of extreme hot weather

e Move and load 25 kg drinking water bottle into dispenser.

k Move barrels from 1st level racking to 3rd level. Each is 120 kg. Should be OK with 3 men. No room for forklift.

Remove refuse bags of broken lab glass to dump. Need it done before end of working day.

b Bring toolboxes 5 x 40 kg through mineshaft 1m x 6m. Tunnels a little flooded so be cautious. Send trainees.

i Load new fire extinguishers 15 kg onto top shelves of storeroom.

h Bring gas cylinders to area 4 immediately. I think they have propane or methane. Bring acid containers also.

Just containers

Objective: To focus on vocabulary to describe different types of containers and their contents.

▶ 1 Find and match

Match the names of the containers (1–15) with the pictures (a–o).

1	crate	_____	**9**	bag
2	box	_____	**10**	bottle
3	sack	_____	**11**	tin
4	case	_____	**12**	packet
5	tube	_____	**13**	drum
6	can	_____	**14**	cylinder
7	pallet	_____	**15**	canister
8	bar	_____		

1 crate _____   **9** bag _____
2 box _____   **10** bottle _____
3 sack _____   **11** tin _____
4 case _____   **12** packet _____
5 tube _____   **13** drum _____
6 can _____   **14** cylinder _____
7 pallet _____   **15** canister _____
8 bar _____

▶ 2 Match and add

Match the containers (1–15) with the typical contents (a–o). There are several possibilities for some items, so be prepared to explain your answers. Then add two more contents from your workplace.

1 crate of _____   **a** soda _____
2 box of _____   **b** cooking gas _____
3 sack of _____   **c** rice _____
4 case of _____   **d** sweets _____
5 tube of _____   **e** water _____
6 can of _____   **f** nuts _____
7 pallet of _____   **g** gas _____
8 bar of _____   **h** bottles _____
9 bag of _____   **i** crude oil _____
10 bottle of _____   **j** boxes _____
11 tin of _____   **k** tuna _____
12 packet of _____   **l** dynamite _____
13 drum of _____   **m** gold _____
14 cylinder of _____   **n** tissues _____
15 canister of _____   **o** hand cream _____

▶ 3 Negotiate a deal

Work in groups of four, two are Team A and two are Team B. Team A want to buy supplies for ZemTeQ and Team B want to sell to ZemTeQ. Both want the best price and conditions. Team A uses the information on page 145 and Team B uses the information on page 146. You have ten minutes to prepare.

6 | Containers: Storeroom madness

Objectives: To review and extend vocabulary for containers. To discuss good and bad housekeeping.

▶ 1 Find 25 differences

Work with a partner. Student A should look at the picture opposite. Student B should look at the picture on page 145. Describe the picture you have to your partner and find the differences between the two pictures. Do not show your picture to your partner. Find 25 differences and label them.

▶ 2 Match the hazards

Match parts A (1–12) and B (a–l) to make poor housekeeping examples from the picture above. Then match them with the hazard C (m–x) they represent to the workers in the area. The first one is done for you.

A	B	C	
1 overturned	a food and drink in room	m dust in work area	1 i p
2 spilt	b tube of glue	n falling objects	
3 left out	c boxes on top shelf	o crushed handling operative	
4 unsealed	d cement bag	p slips by workers	
5 stacked high	e boxes of nails	q explosion near cylinders	
6 left open	f toolbox	r tripping obstacles to staff	
7 cluttered	g acetylene cylinders	s cut hands when opening	
8 dropped	h smoking in room	t skidding by employees	
9 forbidden	i lubricant on floor	u chemical contamination	
10 perched	j oil drum	v harmful fumes to workmen	
11 leaking	k tools on floor	w puncture wounds to workers	
12 uncapped	l water on floor	x animal infestation	

▶ 3 Time to meet

You are going to role-play a safety meeting in groups.

a Look at the items on the agenda and decide what you are going to say.

b Discuss each item in small groups.

c Summarize your discussion for the class.

Agenda

1 Identify all handling jobs in your area.

2 Identify potential container hazards in your area.

3 Identify housekeeping rules to prevent injury with 1 and 2.

Small talk: Requesting and suggesting

Objective: To become more familiar with useful vocabulary and phrases for making requests and suggestions.

In workplace communication it is often necessary to request items and actions, and to make suggestions.

▶ 1 ⓶ 2:3 Listen and write

Listen to the conversation and write the missing words and phrases below.

J Hello, Richard. **1** _____?

R Morning, Jimmy. **2** _____ the door for me, please?

J No problem. You've got a lot of books. **3** _____ help.

R Thanks. **4** _____ the canteen for a coffee? We are very early for class.

J **5** _____. I need something to wake up.

R I had an idea yesterday. **6** _____ organize a class trip to a restaurant? Any **7** _____?

J **8** _____ that fish place by the market in the centre of town. I heard the food is excellent and quite reasonable.

R The **9** _____ is that a lot of people don't like fish. **10** _____ ask people today what they prefer?

J OK. Why don't I **11** _____ later in the week to let you know?

R That would be great. Now, **12** _____ tell me what we did in the last session.

J OK. We talked about ...

A shift leader is talking to a young trainee about the coming week. He asks the trainee to bring several items to the office and then do a series of tasks. He also gives him some suggestions for his first week.

▶ 2 Find and choose

Write 1–12 next to the words and phrases that have a similar meaning to those from the conversation. Use some numbers more than once.

a	shall we stop off at	____	**l**	can I assist you	____
b	only issue	____	**m**	sounds good	____
c	send you an e-mail	____	**n**	could you	____
d	how about we	____	**o**	drawback	____
e	allow me to	____	**p**	how about	____
f	contact you	____	**q**	would you open	____
g	want some help	____	**r**	let's have dinner in	____
h	can you	____	**s**	snag	____
i	leave you a message	____	**t**	ideas	____
j	can you see to	____	**u**	let's pop into	____
k	thoughts	____			

You need some special work done by the workshop. Call them and see if they can do it ASAP. You could make some suggestions as to how they can do the work more quickly and save time for everybody.

▶ 3 Read and speak

With a partner, act out the conversation several times using different words and phrases from Task 2.

You are walking with a friend in the plant. You find an injured worker. Make suggestions about first aid to your friend.

▶ 4 Read and write

a Read the scenarios opposite and choose one.

b With a partner, write out the conversation using words and phrases from Tasks 1 and 2.

c Practise your conversation and then perform it for the class.

You are talking to a classmate about where to go on a class outing with the teacher. Both of you can make suggestions.

Activate your vocabulary
Go to page 152.

Fire safety

1 | Fire quiz

Objective: To practise speaking using key vocabulary connected with fire safety and causes of fire.

▶ 1 Walk and talk

a With a partner, complete the questions below with words from the box.

> drill   blanket   escape   alarm   extinguishers   warn   high-risk
> procedure   officer   training   assembly   types

1 What _____ should you follow if there is a fire?
2 How can you _____ other people if there is a fire?
3 How many classes or _____ of fire are there?
4 Which _____ routes should you use if there is a fire?
5 Where are the nearest fire _____ points?
6 What colour and types of fire _____ do you have in your section?
7 Who is the fire _____ in your section?
8 How often do you have a fire _____?
9 Where are the _____ areas in your company?
10 Do you know what the fire _____ sounds like?
11 What sort of fire _____ does your company give its employees?
12 Do you know how a fire _____ is used to put out a fire?

b Then walk around the class to find out who knows the answers. Try to find at least one student who can answer each question.

▶ 2 Find the words

Try to find eight words and phrases for things that cause fire in the wordsearch on page 146.

▶ 3 Match and write

Match the causes of fire from the wordsearch in Task 2 to the correct examples and definitions below.

1 wiring systems in the plant _____ __
2 bar heater and portable gas heater _____ __
3 discarded cigarettes _____ __
4 cookers and kettles _____ __
5 tools and machines with power cords _____ __
6 boilers and central heating systems _____ __
7 torches, cutters and equipment _____ __
8 wooden sticks used to light cigarettes _____ __

▶ 4 Discuss and rank

With a partner, rank the above causes of fire 1–8, where 1 = most likely to cause a fire and 8 = least likely to cause a fire.

Objective: To review fire safety vocabulary and practise asking about and explaining fire safety signs.

▶ **1** **Describe and match**

Work with a partner. Student A should look at the fire signs below. Student B should look at the fire signs on page 146. Student A describes a sign. Student B finds the sign being described on page 146.

Example: *This sign is diamond-shaped. It is red and has a picture of a flame on it. The word* flammable *is written on the sign.*

▶ **2** **Match the parts**

Jimmy uses ten sentences to explain ten of the signs above.

a Match the sentence halves to make complete sentences.

1 A place where firefighting equipment, __h__ __ll__
2 This person is responsible ____ ____
3 Naked flames are prohibited ____ ____
4 These can often be found in kitchens, ____ ____
5 This information enables you to contact the fire services directly, ____ ____
6 This indicates the escape route in case of fire, ____ ____
7 You should keep this closed so that when there is a fire, ____ ____
8 This is a special fire escape route ____ ____
9 This hydrant sign tells the fire crew or brigade ____ ____
10 Be careful with this material/chemical ____ ____

a and are used to put out small fires.
b and ensures you use the stairs instead of the lift.
c for people with disabilities.
d for organizing fire prevention/firefighting activities.
e and varies from country to country.
f it will not spread.
g in this area.
h such as extinguishers and sand buckets, is kept.
i because it easily catches light and burns.
j where to connect their hoses to a water supply.

b Match each completed sentence with a fire sign.

▶ **3** **Q and As**

a The six questions opposite ask for information you might want to know about the signs. Unscramble them.

b With a partner, point to a sign above and use the questions to ask for information about it.

1 this does what mean?
2 it where I find can?
3 it what is colour?
4 this what does indicate?
5 it big is how?
6 it read should who?

3 | Fire lecture

Objectives: To practise listening for global and detailed information. To become more familiar with language and information about fire types and extinguishers.

▶ 1 ⊚ 2:4 Listen and write

Listen to the first part of Richard's lecture on fire safety and note down your answers to the three questions below.

1 How many general types of fire are there? _____

2 How many B types of fire are there? _____

3 What will they talk about later? _____

▶ 2 ⊚ 2:5 Listen and complete

Listen to the lecture again and complete the table with the missing information. Be warned: one of the boxes is not mentioned in the lecture!

Types of fire	Fires involving	Example extinguishers
A		
	methanol	
		foam
C		
	magnesium, aluminium	
electrical		

▶ 3 Read and complete

What does the colour-coding on a fire extinguisher signify? Use the table above and the e-mails below to complete the missing information.

The extinguishers with a yellow band can be used on type F fires. The extinguishers with a black band can be used on type B and electrical fires. They can't be used in a confined space.

Find out why there is a cream extinguisher in E2. It shouldn't have a foam one.

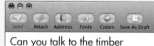

Can you talk to the timber manager about the water extinguishers? They can't be used on flammable liquids or live electrical equipment.

The fire extinguishers with a blue band can be used on several types of fire: A, B, C and electrical fires.

Know your fire extinguisher colour code

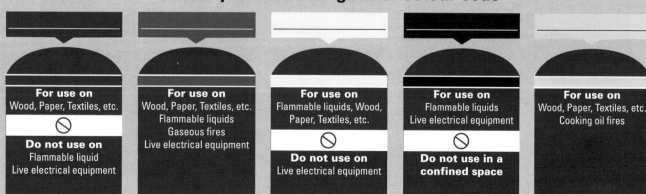

For use on	For use on	For use on	For use on	For use on
Wood, Paper, Textiles, etc.	Wood, Paper, Textiles, etc. Flammable liquids Gaseous fires Live electrical equipment	Flammable liquids, Wood, Paper, Textiles, etc.	Flammable liquids Live electrical equipment	Wood, Paper, Textiles, etc. Cooking oil fires
⊘ Do not use on Flammable liquid Live electrical equipment		⊘ Do not use on Live electrical equipment	⊘ Do not use in a confined space	

Objectives: To identify words and phrases connected with combustion and the fire triangle. To scan-read about different types of fires.

▶ **1   Find and number**

Find the items below in the picture of a ZemTeQ workroom. Write the correct letter next to each item below.

1 ventilation system   _a_
2 books   ___ ___
3 furniture   ___ ___
4 petrol can   ___ ___
5 paint cans   ___ ___
6 oxygen   ___ ___
7 naked flame   ___ ___
8 liquid petroleum gas ___ ___
9 electric bar heater ___ ___
10 overflowing waste bin ___ ___

11 wooden planks   ___ ___
12 cigarettes   ___ ___
13 tube of glue   ___ ___
14 portable grinder   ___ ___
15 packaging materials ___ ___
16 rug   ___ ___
17 matches   ___ ___
18 varnish tin   ___ ___
19 cooker   ___ ___
20 welding equipment   ___ ___

2 Complete the text

Read the text about the fire triangle and complete it using the words in the box.

There are three things needed for 1 _____ to happen. The first is a 2 _____ that burns. This could include small pieces of 3 _____ like wood chips, liquids like 4 _____ and/or 5 _____ such as propane. The second is an 6 _____ supply. This can be from air (which has 20% oxygen), or given off by oxidizing chemicals. The final one is a source of 7 _____. This raises the temperature above the ignition point. This can include a hot 8 _____, electrical equipment, static 9 _____ or a naked 10 _____.

gases   ignition
oxygen   fuel   electricity
flame   solids   petrol
combustion   surface

3 Discuss the dangers in the picture

a Look at the items from Task 1 and write a letter next to each one: **F** if they are a fuel; **O** if they are a source of oxygen and **I** if they are a source of ignition.
b Which things are the most likely to cause a serious fire?
c What type of fire extinguishers would be needed to extinguish a fire in the workshop?

4 Scan the extracts

The extracts below are from *ZemTeQ News*. They are about fires at ZemTeQ over the last 12 months.

1 How many words/phrases can you find meaning *fire*?
2 How many words/phrases can you find meaning *caused by*?
3 How many words/phrases can you find meaning *damaged*?

a
Acetone up in Flames
A fire incinerated containers of acetone in storage B5 area. An unknown number of people are missing as officers declared the source was probably a blowtorch left on.

b
Blaze Guts Tanks 4 & 5
One person suffered 1st degree burns as a blaze gutted fuel tanks 4 and 5. Firefighters blamed it on arson.

c
Hot Metal Still Alight
Flames burned the warehouse storage for Mg and Al in ZemTeQ G3 area. Officials pointed the finger at thrown away matches in the trash. A couple of people are believed dead.

d
Inferno Ruins Fat Store
An inferno ruined the storage for drums of fat for cooking industry. Authorities stated it was due to a faulty fuse box. One fatality was reported.

e
Lights Out for ZemTeQ
A huge blaze demolished the frame of the electricity generating building A6. Inspectors announced it came about because of a lightning strike. Three fatalities due to smoke inhalation resulted.

f
Bang! Propane Goes Up
Members of the police force commented that fire resulted from a malfunctioning bar heater after the inferno scorched the propane storage area C2. Twelve nearby workers were lucky to escape injury.

Look at the extracts one by one as a class and predict what the rest of the article will say.

5 Read and check

With a partner, read through the headlines and answer the following questions for each one. Then check as a class.

1 What damage was done by the fire?
2 What deaths or injuries did the fire cause?
3 What caused the fire?
4 What class of fire was it and what extinguisher would you use?

Objective: To practise using ordinal numbers in the context of dates.

▶ 1 Unscramble and match

a Unscramble the words below. They are ordinal numbers, dates and/or floors in a building.

1 stirf   _FIRST_   _1st_   _f_

2 donces   _____ _____ ___

3 vheenst   _____ _____ ___

4 hettn   _____ _____ ___

5 tiffh   _____ _____ ___

6 hfturo   _____ _____ ___

7 tinnh   _____ _____ ___

8 githeh   _____ _____ ___

9 hridt   _____ _____ ___

10 hixst   _____ _____ ___

b Write the numerical form next to each word.

c Match each word with a picture opposite (a–j).

▶ 2 Share your dates

It is Fire Check Month for Jimmy. His boss has written him a memo giving him instructions for the month. There are a few items missing.

a Work with a partner. Student A should read the information below and Student B should read the information on page 147.

b Ask each other questions and exchange information to complete the gaps in your memos.

> On the 3rd and 4th, you need to check the _____; meet with me on the last Friday of the month to talk about it. On _____ you must do a fire alarm drill, but not on the _____ because you should inspect the fire hoses. On the 17th, talk to the _____ and on the 7th, to the _____ about car parking. On the second _____ and the _____, check with the shift supervisor about the new assembly points. The day after the hose check, see me about _____. There is also a firefighters' meeting the _____ the last fire drill. Take the first two Sundays off and the last two Saturdays. The _____ Mondays, check the fire trucks are OK. The day after the second truck check, ask Richard to do the _____. You're free the other days for _____.

▶ 3 Exchange information

Complete the diary planner on page 147 and compare it with your partner's to see if you have exchanged information correctly. Then check as a class.

6 Escape plan

Objective: To review language for the procedure of reporting a fire or evacuating a building.

▶ 1 Read and complete

Read the ZemTeQ Fire Action poster that explains the procedure for escape from and reporting a fire. Match the gaps (1–15) in the poster with the words and phrases (a–o) below.

a number
b dial
c building
d run
e action

f assembly point
g address
h alarm
i lift
j safe

k fire
l discover
m risk
n fire brigade
o personal items

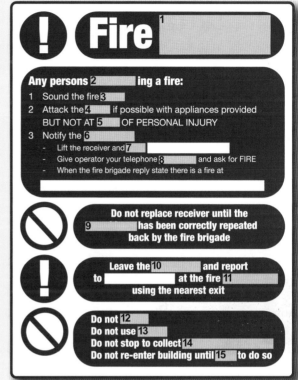

! Fire 1

Any persons 2 _____ ing a fire:

1 Sound the fire 3 ___
2 Attack the 4 ___ if possible with appliances provided BUT NOT AT 5 ___ OF PERSONAL INJURY
3 Notify the 6 ___
 - Lift the receiver and 7 ___
 - Give operator your telephone 8 ___ and ask for FIRE
 - When the fire brigade reply state there is a fire at

Do not replace receiver until the 9 ___ has been correctly repeated back by the fire brigade

Leave the 10 ___ and report to ___ at the fire 11 ___ using the nearest exit

Do not 12 ___
Do not use 13 ___
Do not stop to collect 14 ___
Do not re-enter building until 15 ___ to do so

▶ 2 Write and ask

a Use some of the words from Task 1 to complete the questions below.

1 At what _____ do you meet if there is a fire?

2 How often have you heard the _____?

3 How long does it take the _____ to come?

4 Have you ever been trapped in a _____?

5 What _____ do you _____ to call the firefighters?

6 What is the fire _____ procedure in your section?

7 Have you ever _____ed a fire at work or home?

8 What is the postal _____ of your section or area?

9 Do you _____ if you hear the alarm?

10 What _____ do you keep at work?

11 Is it _____ to go in a burning _____ to rescue a buddy?

12 Is a BBQ a high-, medium- or low- _____ fire?

13 What building has had the most _____s on site?

b Ask and discuss the questions in groups.

▶ 3 Find the exit

The alarm has sounded. Jimmy is just inside the warehouse. He follows the route shown by the dotted line. Look at the patterns of his route so far and decide how Jimmy will complete the route. Say which Fire Assembly Point he must go to (A–L).

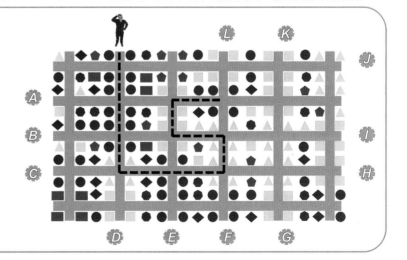

Small talk: Pros and cons

Objective: To become more familiar with useful vocabulary and phrases for talking about the pros and cons of a situation.

To make good decisions in the workplace, we need to think about and talk about both the advantages and disadvantages of a situation or an item.

▶ 1 🔊 2:6 Listen and write

Listen to the conversation and write the missing words and phrases below.

J Hi, Richard. Can I 1 _____ you? I need some advice.

R Oh, hi, Jimmy. Sure. 2 _____?

J I'm not sure what to do. I have been offered two 3 _____, one in the health and safety office and the other as part of the investigation team on site. Which is better?

R Well, I think both have a lot of 4 _____. A big 5 _____ for the office is that it's safe, clean and comfortable. 6 _____, it can be boring if you're an active person.

J Yeah, 7 _____. I like walking round the site and chatting to the guys. But it's not so good in bad weather.

R Yes, but 8 _____, the outdoor job will be different every day. It will be more interesting.

J I guess. I need to 9 _____.

R Good idea. Why not write two lists? Write the 10 _____ and 11 _____ and then decide.

J Thanks, Richard. I 12 _____ your advice.

▶ 2 Find and choose

Write 1–12 next to the words and phrases that have a similar meaning to those from the conversation. Use some numbers more than once.

a	have a word with	____	**m** am thankful for	____
b	in general	____	**n** negatives	____
c	cons	____	**o** pluses	____
d	positions	____	**p** am grateful for	____
e	good points	____	**q** having said that	____
f	consider the pros and cons	____	**r** basically	____
g	is there a problem	____	**s** posts	____
h	pros	____	**t** you're right	____
i	advantage	____	**u** then again	____
j	even so	____	**v** positives	____
k	weigh it up	____	**w** mull it over	____
l	anything wrong	____	**x** speak to	____

▶ 3 Read and speak

With a partner, act out the conversation several times using different words and phrases from Task 2.

▶ 4 Read and write

a Read the scenarios opposite and choose one.

b With a partner, write out the conversation using words and phrases from Tasks 1 and 2.

c Practise your conversation and then perform it for the class.

You are with a friend in a car showroom weighing up the pluses and minuses of two makes of car before you go ahead and buy one.

There is a health and safety meeting regarding PPE items used in your section. Two of the workers in the meeting start to argue about the pros and cons of various items of PPE.

Classmates are discussing the pros and cons of restaurants around town to which they want to take the teacher. Make sure you consider everything.

Two shift leaders discuss the good and bad points of working on both the night and day shifts in the factory or other parts of the plant.

Co-workers are talking about transferring to other departments and so chat about the advantages and disadvantages of various jobs.

Activate your vocabulary
Go to page 152.

Chemical safety and hazardous substances

1 Hazchem quiz

Objective: To review hazchem vocabulary and practise speaking about chemicals in the workplace.

C	I	C	B	B	U	R	N
D	T	O	C	R	A	C	K
O	C	M	S	C	Y	I	C
A	H	B	T	O	A	R	P
L	Y	U	O	D	V	R	O
Q	G	S	R	A	A	I	I
S	M	T	E	M	P	T	S
E	D	T	A	A	O	A	O
A	X	I	G	G	U	T	N
V	R	P	S	E	R	E	U
O	E	B	L	P	F	X	P
I	A	I	Z	O	O	H	N
D	C	I	N	D	D	S	X
W	T	Y	M	H	I	E	E
O	C	O	N	T	A	C	T
G	V	I	R	N	G	L	C
M	L	A	B	E	L	U	E
S	W	A	L	L	O	W	U
I	N	F	L	A	M	E	G
H	A	R	M	W	E	A	R

▶ 1 Find the words

Try to find 20 words connected with chemical hazards in the wordsearch. Write them in the spaces below in alphabetical order.

_____   _____   _____

_____   _____   _____

_____   _____   _____

_____   _____   _____

_____   _____   _____

_____   _____   _____

_____   _____

▶ 2 Test each other

With a partner, test each other on the words in Task 1 using the four questions below.

1 How do you spell X?   3 How do you say X?
2 What does X mean?   4 Can you give me a sentence with X?

▶ 3 Walk and talk

a With a partner, complete the questions below with some of the words from Task 1.

1 Does your skin _____ to any chemicals or substances?

2 How do you get rid of or _____ of unwanted substances at home?

3 Do you _____ PPE for any substances at home and work?

4 What hazardous substances do you come into _____ with at work?

5 What substances can harm or _____ your car?

6 What substances can singe or _____ skin at work?

7 What makes your skin split or _____?

8 What items easily _____ in your home?

9 What would you do if you _____ed a dangerous substance?

10 What substances do you _____ under your sink at home?

11 What annoys or _____ you?

12 Can you name three local _____ous animals?

13 What makes you scratch and _____?

14 What substances do you stay away from or _____, and why?

15 Can you describe a sticker or _____ on a chemical at work?

b Then walk around the class to find out who knows the answers. Try to find at least one student who can answer each question.

Objectives: To practise listening for detailed information. To complete a table with information about hazardous chemicals.

▶ **1** ☉ **2:7 Listen and write**

Listen to Richard's lecture on hazardous materials at ZemTeQ. Note down your answers to the three questions below.

1 How are hazardous substances generally categorized? _____

2 Which is the most common type of hazardous substance found at ZemTeQ?

_____

3 Where can you find out about other types of hazardous substances at ZemTeQ?

_____

▶ **2** ☉ **2:8 Listen and complete**

Listen to the lecture again and complete the table with the missing information.

	Examples	Injuries	Sign
Explosive/ flammable	Organic solvents and petroleum		
Harmful		Limited health risks	
Irritant			
Corrosive			
Toxic		Stop body functions like heart, kidney, liver	
Carcinogen			
Other		Not mentioned	

▶ **3** **Look and match**

Look at the signs on page 148. Decide which sign goes with each category in the table. (There is no sign for one category.)

▶ **4** **Read and decide**

Read the incident reports and decide what type of substance each one is describing. Discuss your ideas with a partner.

Incident 1
A worker complained of redness and inflammation on his hands and itching all over his body after working with substance A; the exposure time was low and it may be an allergic reaction.

Incident 2
Contact with substance B led to third degree wounds on hands and arms resulting from a spillage. They are serious injuries that look like scalding marks. The substance ate away clothing also.

Incident 3
The worker breathed in substance C, which left him dizzy and faint. The injury is short-term and not serious. Inspection showed that the injury was avoidable with correct PPE. The worker has received a warning.

Objectives: To complete a problem-solving task involving reading and discussion. To review prepositions and language for hazards.

▶ 1   Solve the puzzle

Jimmy has a problem. There are 14 barrels of chemicals he has to store correctly. The current storage system is very dangerous and there have been a few incidents. He must read the 16 pieces of information so he can label and put the barrels A–L and X–Y in their correct storage bay below.

a   Read the 16 pieces of information about the barrels.

1   X and Y should be as far apart as possible, as they are explosive together.
2   Barrels of the same colour should not be directly opposite or next to each other.
3   A corrosive chemical cannot be placed next to another corrosive chemical in this store.
4   A, H and L are very safe together and must be located side by side.
5   X, A, D, E, F, I and K are all corrosive.
6   Y, B, C, G, H, J and L are all non-corrosive.
7   L and E are volatile together.
8   X and G instantly combust when situated adjacently.
9   Y and I are hazardous when stored in neighbouring spots.
10   F and E can be put opposite each other safely.
11   K and B can be stored beside each other.
12   B can be hazardous near other red family chemicals, but can be in the vicinity of A.
13   D and J can be stored beside one another.
14   E and Y are compatible when next to one another.
15   L and J are OK to store opposite each other.
16   B is good to separate D and K.

b   Decide the order in which the barrels should be stored. Work in groups.

▶ 2   Chat and find

With a partner, find one or more words and phrases from the rules in Task 1 that mean the same as 1–9 below.

1   near _____
2   next to _____
3   located _____
4   dangerous _____
5   unstable _____
6   stable _____
7   keep apart _____
8   immediately _____
9   catch fire _____

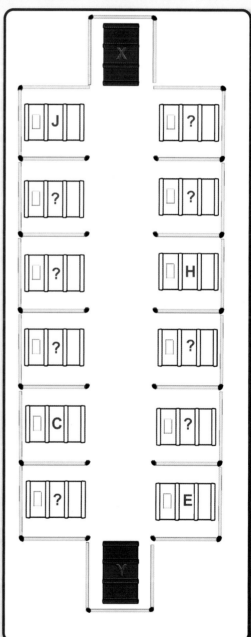

Objectives: To focus on key words connected with hazchem precautions.
To practise careful reading.

▶ 1 Read and sort

a Read the account below of safety measures that were covered during a trainee tour last week. Check you understand the words in italics.

> The hazmat trainer, Dave, started the tour talking about *PPE* and then the *substitution* of materials for less hazardous ones. After that, he showed trainees how to use a hood for *local exhaust ventilation*, and then went on to *containment* and keeping the work in a specific area. Next, he went through *personal hygiene* in the washroom and then how to reduce the *number of employees* in the workspace. At the seventh stop, he noted the importance of *cleaning up* spills immediately, and later *general ventilation* for work areas. *Reducing exposure time* was next on the tour, followed by how to *separate incompatible materials* for safety.

b Put the pictures opposite in the correct order.

▶ 2 Label the pictures

Label the pictures opposite with the words below. Use each word as many times as you like.

> door   temperature   ventilation system   keep-clear area   sink   switch
> dizzy   vacuum   clock   broom   bucket   welding   window   cubicle   workers
> mask   cylinder   goggles   gloves   pipe   sweat   mirror   spillage
> cupboard   mop   walkway   toilet   basin   shelves   drum   tap

▶ 3 Read and match

Look at Dave's descriptions of the ten precautions in italics in Task 1. Label each description with the correct precaution name.

1

This substance must be kept in a restricted area to reduce its spread and exposure to workers.

2

Chemical-handling workmen need to use special gear when exposure cannot be controlled by other measures, to protect workers from inhalation, ingestion and direct contact.

3

Trained personnel need to use the extraction system to suck away dust, fumes and gases or vapour in order to reduce the exposure of workers to unfiltered air.

4

There must be correct cleaning equipment to hand for spillages for cleaning department members to use, such as mops, brooms and vacuums, to prevent exposure to workers.

5

Limit the time workers are in contact with the substance. Each substance has a set limit; beyond this limit is normally hazardous.

6

Incompatible materials are to be kept apart in every part of the storage warehouse to reduce the risk of substances reacting with each other.

7

All over plant cleaning staff must replace the cleaning solution with one that is less hazardous to workers. It must still clean and needs doing immediately.

8

The operatives in loading areas must keep and use substances away from co-workers to lower exposure to chemicals and reduce the risk to employees, especially when a delivery comes.

9

All new operators who come on shift must use washing and cleaning facilities to scrub up before they eat, drink or smoke, to stop contamination by ingestion or skin contact.

10

When using the substance, always make sure there is a supply of fresh air by fan or power ventilation system.

_____
_____

_____
_____

_____
_____

_____
_____

_____
_____

_____
_____

_____
_____

_____
_____

_____
_____

_____
_____

Unit 10 Chemical safety and hazardous substances

Objective: To become more familiar with the language used for labelling hazardous substances and practise scanning safety labels.

Labels are an important way for workers to identify substances. They contain information, including the substance name, risks and safety precautions. Can you remember what is written on the labels of substances you use?

▶ **1 Answer the questions**

Look at the chemical labels and answer the questions below.

1 What are the names of the substances?
2 What symbols are shown for each?
3 Which is toxic if breathed in?
4 Which is ignited by static electricity?
5 Which can kill fish?
6 Which needs to be stored where there is plenty of air?
7 Which needs to be locked up?
8 Which needs PPE for the hands?
9 Which is poisonous if ingested?
10 Where are they produced?

Corrosive

Heavy Duty Cleaner

Avoid contact with skin and eyes. In case of contact with skin and eyes, rinse immediately with plenty of water and seek medical advice. Wear suitable protective clothing, gloves and eye/face protection. In case of accident or if you feel unwell, seek medical advice immediately – show label if possible.

ZemTeQ Chemicals, Eastern Division, ZemTeQ City

Glutaraldehyde

Toxic by inhalation and if swallowed. Causes burns. May cause sensitization by inhalation and by skin contact. Very toxic to aquatic organisms. Keep locked up and out of reach of children. In case of contact with eyes, rinse immediately with plenty of water and seek medical advice. Wear suitable protective clothing, gloves and eye/face protection. In case of accident or if you feel unwell, seek medical advice immediately – show label if possible. Avoid release to the environment. Refer to special instructions/safety data sheet.

Toxic

Dangerous for the environment

ZemTeQ Chemicals, Eastern Division, ZemTeQ City

Highly flammable

Acetone

Highly flammable. Keep container in a well-ventilated place. Keep away from sources of ignition. No smoking. Do not breathe gas/fumes/vapour/spray. Take measures against static discharges.

ZemTeQ Chemicals, Eastern Division, ZemTeQ City

▶ 2 **Find and match**

Find words and phrases in the risk and safety phrase boxes similar to the words and phrases below each box.

Label Risk Phrases

4 Highly flammable

14 TOXIC TO FAUNA

11 Repeated exposure may cause lung damage

9 **Irritating to eyes**

1 Explosive when dry

12 Contact with water liberates toxic gas

2 Risk of explosion by shock, friction or fire

13 May cause cancer

8 Irritating to respiratory system

10 Toxic to flora

15 Vapours may cause drowsiness and dizziness

7 **Harmful in contact with skin**

6 Harmful if swallowed

3 May cause fire

5 Extremely flammable

a jolt	**c** gives off	**e** ingested	**g** can	**i** animals
b breathing	**d** sleepiness	**f** dehydrated	**h** plants	**j** subjection

Label Safety Phrases

23 Dispose of this material and its container at hazardous or special waste collection point

20 **Wear face protection**

16 Keep away from sources of ignition – no smoking

18 Avoid contact with the skin

24 If swallowed, rinse mouth with water if conscious

22 Keep temperature at not exceeding 52°C

19 Never add water to this product

25 Use only in well-ventilated areas

17 **Keep container dry**

21 In case of accident by inhalation, remove casualty to fresh air and keep at rest

k maintain	**n** work with solely	**q** do not let it near
l steer clear of	**o** get rid of	**r** no more than
m on no account	**p** put on	

▶ 3 **Give safety advice**

In groups, think of a hazardous substance you use and discuss the safety precautions needed when it is used.

Objectives: To complete a problem-solving task using words and phrases from Lesson 5. To write a safety label using language from the unit.

▶ **1** **Talk and solve**

Jimmy has been asked to make labels for five substances. He must ask the workers in Area 5 in the chemical plant about the risk and safety phrases for each, so he can make the labels. Each substance has three risk phrases, one each from parts I, II and III. Also, each substance has two safety phrases, one each from parts IV and V. All are from 1–25 of the phrases from Lesson 5, Task 2.

a Choose a worker name below (Andy, etc.) and go to page 147 to find out what that person said. Copy only what your worker said onto the correct line below.

b Walk around the class exchanging information. Write the other workers' information.

c When you have all the information, work with a partner and complete the answer grid.

Andy	*Substance V makes you yawn and feel dizzy.*
Randy	
Sandy	
Pete	
Dean	
Owen	
John	
Jean-Paul	
Ian	
Jack	
Johnny	
Wally	
Jacques	
Jeremy	

Hazardous substances	Risk phrases I-III															Safety phrases IV–V									
	Part I					Part II					Part III					Part IV					Part V				
	1	2	3	4	5	6	7	8	9	10	11	12	13	14	15	16	17	18	19	20	21	22	23	24	25
Substance V											✗	✗	✗	✗	✓										
Substance W															✗										
Substance X															✗										
Substance Y															✗										
Substance Z															✗										

▶ 2 **Draw the labels**

When you have solved the puzzle, draw all five labels with the correct phrases.

▶ 3 **Give safety advice**

a Write safety labels for a hazardous substance you know or use, using the prompts below.

1 Keep away from ...

2 Keep container ...

3 Avoid ...

4 Never ...

5 Wear ...

6 In case of ...

7 Keep temperature ...

8 Dispose of ...

9 If swallowed ...

10 Use only ...

b Read your sentences to the class to see if they can guess what the substance is.

Objective: To become more familiar with useful vocabulary and phrases for asking for and giving advice in English.

We ask for and give advice all the time in the workplace so that we can do our jobs better and improve communication.

▶ **1** 🎧 **2:9 Listen and write**

Listen to the conversation and write the missing words and phrases below.

J Richard, hello. I'm **1** _____.

R Morning, Jimmy. What's the problem?

J Well, I've locked my keys in the car with my books and the important report my **2** _____ wants to see today. What an idiot I am! What should I do?

R **3** _____. Why not call home for **4** _____ key?

J Nobody's home. And my mobile's in the car.

R OK. **5** _____ explain to your boss and tell him you will bring it tomorrow.

J No way. He will kill me. He's going to **6** _____ me for this.

R No he won't. Look, I have **7** _____. I have a hammer in my car. I will **8** _____ the window and you can get it repaired in ZemTeQ's vehicle repair centre later.

J **9** _____. I suppose there isn't another **10** _____. Which car park are you in?

▶ **2** **Find and choose**

Write 1–10 next to the words and phrases that have a similar meaning to those from the conversation. Use some numbers more than once.

a	in trouble	____	**l**	you ought to	____
b	you're right	____	**m**	break	____
c	a back-up	____	**n**	gaffer	____
d	method	____	**o**	in a spot of bother	____
e	give me the boot	____	**p**	option	____
f	choice	____	**q**	relax	____
g	take a deep breath	____	**r**	sack	____
h	the answer	____	**s**	an extra	____
i	chief	____	**t**	I'll do that	____
j	a second	____	**u**	manager	____
k	it	____			

▶ **3** **Read and speak**

With a partner, act out the conversation several times using different words and phrases from Task 2.

▶ **4** **Read and write**

a Read the scenarios opposite and choose one.

b With a partner, write out the conversation using words and phrases from Tasks 1 and 2.

c Practise your conversation and then perform it for the class.

A worker is having problems with his boss, who he thinks doesn't like him because he gives him bad jobs. He asks his friend for advice.

You have been offered a job in another company. The salary is better than your current one. But it's dirtier and longer hours. You ask for advice from your shift manager.

You have had a bad back injury at work. You go to the medical centre to talk about it with the doctor there. He gives you lots of good advice.

You find an envelope in the street with a large amount of money in it. Call a friend to ask for advice about what to do.

You see another student cheat in an exam, so you talk to a friend for advice about what to do.

Activate your vocabulary

Go to page 152.

Electrical safety

1 | Electricity dangers lecture

Objective: To learn some key terms connected with electricity and to listen for both gist and detail in the context of the dangers of electricity.

▶ 1 ⊙ 2:10 Listen and write

You are going to listen to Richard's lecture on the dangers of electricity and complete the table opposite. Listen a second time if necessary.

	Danger	What is it?	Leads to what?
1		Electricity flowing through the body	
2			
3	Arc eye		
4			25% of ZemTeQ fires
5			

▶ 2 ⊙ 2:11 Listen for key words

Richard's lecture contains many questions about electrical safety. Listen to it again and complete the sentences below.

1 Is the cable _____ clamped? ____
2 Did you inspect it? ____
3 Who inspected the equipment? ____
4 Is it in good condition? ____
5 Do you know about _____ connections? ____
6 What is a _____? ____
7 What's an _____? ____
8 Does it have an inspection _____ tag? ____
9 Is it _____ properly? ____
10 Is it flexible? ____
11 How do you know? ____
12 What's double _____? ____
13 What _____ does it have? ____
14 Is it suitable? ____
15 Is it in good condition? ____

▶ 3 ⊙ 2:12 Listen and categorize

Listen to the lecture one more time and decide what each question is asking about. Mark each question **S** for supply, **E** for equipment, **P** for plugs, **C** for cables, **A** for appliances or **I** for inspection.

▶ 4 Practise key language

a Work with a partner. Write a dialogue between two workers about the electrical safety of a tool in your area. Include questions from Task 2.

b Practise your dialogue and then perform it for the class without your script.

Objective: To read about and discuss how electric shocks should be avoided and dealt with.

▶ **1**   **Read and think**

Look at the electric shock poster below and guess some of the missing words.

In Case of Shock

1   Raise the **1** _____ by calling for **2** _____ from colleagues.
    Make sure someone notifies a **3** _____.

2   **4** _____ power if isolation **5** _____ position known.

3   Call for an **6** _____.

4   If not possible to switch off power, **7** _____ electrocution.
    – Push/pull person away from conductor
    – Use an object made from good **8** _____ (e.g., **9** _____ chair/broom)
    – Stand on dry **10** _____ material (newspaper/**11** _____ mat)

5   Check for **12** _____. If yes, put in **13** _____ position so
    14 _____ is open.

6   If not breathing, apply **15** _____ resuscitation. If no pulse,
    try **16** _____.

▶ **2**   **Look and write**

Find the 16 words or phrases from Task 1 in the wordsearch.

A	A	W	O	O	D	E	N	H	E	L	P	M	O	U	T	H	T	O	M	O	U	T	H	O
L	J	V	V	U	G	T	I	N	S	U	L	A	T	I	N	G	Y	F	C	P	R	K	H	I
A	N	T	O	R	E	C	O	V	E	R	Y	I	P	T	P	G	S	P	R	U	B	B	E	R
R	Q	Z	Z	I	B	Q	X	Q	I	N	S	U	L	A	T	O	R	A	X	B	M	P	F	E
M	T	O	J	K	D	F	I	R	S	T	A	I	D	E	R	B	S	L	G	S	Z	Q	M	I
S	W	I	T	C	H	K	Q	B	R	E	A	T	H	I	N	G	N	A	I	R	W	A	Y	U
X	D	H	A	M	B	U	L	A	N	C	E	F	T	S	W	I	T	C	H	O	F	F	S	G

▶ **3**   **Discuss and answer**

a   Answer questions 1–10, in small groups.

   1 How can you avoid electrocution?

   2 Why switch off the power?

   3 What is the recovery position?

   4 What is CPR and when and why do you use it?

   5 How can you check for breathing?

   6 Why use a wooden chair?

   7 Why stand on a newspaper?

   8 What other insulating materials could you use?

   9 Have you ever been electrocuted? What happened?

   10 How do you raise the alarm in your section?

b   Now discuss these points about your workplace in the same groups.

3 | Electric shock dilemma maze

Objective: To read information and make decisions that solve a problem.

▶ 1 Read, listen and decide

Work in groups of three. Take it in turns to read out the situation in each step and decide what to do. Find your way out of the maze by answering correctly.

Situation: You are an employee of ZemTeQ and are crossing the yard on your way to the office. **Start at 1.**

1 In the yard, you see an unconscious man near power cables and a power tool with an extension cord. Do you:
a call for help? **Go to 2**
b unplug the machine? **Go to 8**
c check his pulse? **Go to 15**

2 You are not able to switch off the power on the tool. A workmate says he has called an ambulance. Do you try to move the victim away from the tool by:
a fetching a broom to push or pull him away? **Go to 7**
b grabbing him quickly to pull him away? **Go to 32**
c using a metal rod to move him away? **Go to 30**

3 The victim begins to recover, but his colour changes. You leave to get an ambulance. **Go to 32**

4 You try two breaths to resuscitate the victim, but the victim doesn't start breathing. Do you pump:
a in the middle of his chest? **Go to 23**
b on the left side of his chest? **Go to 27**

5 You're not sure of CPR because you haven't done training.
a You try to remember CPR from TV. **Go to 33**
b Jimmy arrives and wants to help you. **Go to 19**
c You manage to stay calm. You hope an ambulance comes quickly. **Go to 21**

6 A friend shouts: 'What are you doing? Check his signs and get a first aider'. Do you:
a examine the injured man? **Go to 8**
b tell a friend to go and find a first aider? **Go to 18**

7 You see several brooms available. Do you choose:
a a metal one? **Go to 32**
b a wooden one? **Go to 13**

8 You see the victim has body burns. Do you:
a wrap them with wet bandages? **Go to 21**
b apply a dry bandage? **Go to 19**
c take no action? **Go to 24**

9 This is not an option. You must take control. **Go to 21**

10 His mobile rings. It's for him. You put it to his ear. **Go to 28**

11 The victim dies. Ask yourself why. **Go to 1**

12 This doesn't work. The victim seems worse. Do you:
a unplug the tool in his hand? **Go to 2**
b sprinkle water on him? **Go to 6**

13 You need to touch the victim with the broom, but also insulate yourself. Do you:
a stand on a pallet? **Go to 17**
b stay on the floor? **Go to 25**

14 The victim looks much better and you want to make sure he is comfortable. Do you:
a light a cigarette for him? **Go to 26**
b watch his vital signs? **Go to 25**
c give him a cup of tea? **Go to 3**

15 You have risked your own life, but his pulse is still not good. Do you now:
a perform mouth-to-mouth? **Go to 12**
b try CPR? **Go to 5**
c move him to the recovery position? **Go to 19**

16 The first aider arrives. He cannot believe how many mistakes you have made. You need training. **Go to 11**

17 You manage to pull him clear, but he is not breathing properly. Do you:
a slap his face to resuscitate him? **Go to 22**
b put him in the recovery position? **Go to 20**
c stop and think what to do? **Go to 24**

18 The victim is recovering. Well done. But you must get some CPR and first-aid training.

19 The injured man speaks. He says he is in pain. Do you:
a apply some ointment? **Go to 12**
b offer him a painkiller? **Go to 32**

20 He opens his mouth and regains consciousness. **Go to 14**

21 The victim looks worse, so you must do something quickly. Do you:
a continue to wait for help? **Go to 9**
b run and get help? **Go to 31**

22 He looks drowsy. You slap him gently. **Go to 26**

23 He whispers something in your ear – he's in pain.
a You reassure him that everything will be fine. **Go to 16**
b You give him some medicine. **Go to 11**

24 His colour gets worse. Do you:
a throw water on him? **Go to 29**
b roll him onto his stomach? **Go to 6**

25 You remember your health and safety training. You need to stand on something.
a You use a rubber mat. **Go to 17**
b You use a drain cover. **Go to 32**

26 His breathing improves a little. You give him some food. **Go to 32**

27 You need to learn CPR. This has cost a life. **Go to 32**

28 He opens his eyes a little. He feels cold. Do you:
a put a blanket over him? **Go to 2**
b loosen his overalls to cool him down? **Go to 12**

29 This makes things much worse. Do you now:
a position him on his back? **Go to 6**
b lay him on his side? **Go to 36**

30 You remember some training. The rod might conduct electricity so you get a shock. Do you:
a try to hook him with the rod? **Go to 34**
b decide to use a metal stepladder instead? **Go to 6**

31 You get back quickly and he asks for food. Do you:
a give him your sandwich? **Go to 32**
b ignore him and check his pulse and breathing? **Go to 28**
c tell him he can eat soon? **Go to 12**

32 This results in death. Decide why and explain to your teacher. **Go to 1**

33 He looks pale. You don't know what you are doing! Do you:
a tilt his head back and listen for breathing? **Go to 4**
b bang on his chest? **Go to 12**

34 He looks brighter. You make him stand up and walk. **Go to 32**

35 He has a regular pulse, but is short of breath. Do you:
a think about calling an ambulance? **Go to 3**
b get him some food? **Go to 26**
c make him stand and walk? **Go to 34**
d slap his face gently? **Go to 22**
e inspect the tool to find the problem? **Go to 32**
f stay and watch only? **Go to 18**

36 You are doing better. This looks like the recovery position. Do you now:
a put him on a stretcher? **Go to 10**
b keep talking to him? **Go to 19**

Objective: To practise using comparatives.

▶ 1 Discuss the sentences

Look at these sentences. Which **one** is grammatically correct, but factually wrong, and which **one** is both grammatically and factually correct?

1 China is more big than the USA.
2 The USA is biggest than China.
3 China is bigger than the USA.
4 The USA is big than China.
5 The USA is bigger than China.
6 The USA is more big than China.
7 China is big than the USA.
8 China is biggest than the USA.

▶ 2 Look and speak

Work with a partner. Make comparative sentences using one word or phrase from each circle. Then check as a whole class to see if any pairs said the same thing.

A

hot old
refreshing
difficult cold
RELAXING DEEP
fit hard-working expensive
new long fast
TIRING loud
delicious
high far away
big

B

China
platinum
Stonehenge Jupiter
FIREWORKS Nile
office manager English
bicycle iPods
Coca-Cola
WORKING
Mt Kilimanjaro home
desert snow
swimmer rice
Atlantic

C

ice
PYRAMID
cheetah Chinese
pasta USA operative
footballer beach
Pepsi jungle Saturn
plasma TV
shopping gold
Amazon Pacific
Mt Fuji gun

▶ 3 Practise writing

Choose ten of the comparative sentences that you invented for Task 2 and write them in the spaces below. Then exchange your sentences with a partner and make any necessary corrections.

1 _____
2 _____
3 _____
4 _____
5 _____
6 _____
7 _____
8 _____
9 _____
10 _____

5 Comparatives 2

Objective: To review comparatives.

▶ 1 Look and talk

Work with a partner. Look at the list of adjectives below and discuss what each means.

a toxic	**g** messy	**m** cheap	**s** accident-prone
b easy-to-use	**h** noisy	**n** cold	**t** corrosive
c ventilated	**i** accessible	**o** friendly	**u** disposable
d reliable	**j** punctual	**p** waterproof	**v** insulated
e hard	**k** conductive	**q** reactive	**w** organized
f flexible	**l** flammable	**r** dirty	**x** helpful

▶ 2 Think and choose

Work with the same partner. Write the opposite of each adjective in Task 1 in the space next to it. Use the prefixes below in some cases, and in other cases, use a completely new word. Two of the adjectives do not have opposites.

> in~   non~   un~   dis~

Examples: *reliable → unreliable*   *hard → soft*

▶ 3 Ten-in-a-row

You are going to play a game in teams of four. The aim is to get ten boxes in a row on the grid below. You win a box by giving a comparative sentence that is correct (factually and grammatically), using an adjective from Task 1. Your group must accept the sentence.

	People					Places					Tools					Substances					Materials				
	Teacher	The first aider	My boss	Classmate	Me	Canteen	Warehouse	Workshop	Office	WC	Hammer	Saw	Drill	Welding gear	Lathe	Water	Oil	Petrol	Lubricant	Cleaning fluid	Wood	Steel	Plastic	Iron	MDF
Materials — MDF	A1	A2	A3	A4	A5	A6	A7	A8	A9	A10	A11	A12	A13	A14	A15	A16	A17	A18	A19	A20	A21	A22	A23	A24	
Iron	B1	B2	B3	B4	B5	B6	B7	B8	B9	B10	B11	B12	B13	B14	B15	B16	B17	B18	B19	B20	B21	B22	B23		B25
Plastic	C1	C2	C3	C4	C5	C6	C7	C8	C9	C10	C11	C12	C13	C14	C15	C16	C17	C18	C19	C20	C21	C22		C24	C25
Steel	D1	D2	D3	D4	D5	D6	D7	D8	D9	D10	D11	D12	D13	D14	D15	D16	D17	D18	D19	D20	D21		D23	D24	D25
Wood	E1	E2	E3	E4	E5	E6	E7	E8	E9	E10	E11	E12	E13	E14	E15	E16	E17	E18	E19	E20		E22	E23	E24	E25
Substances — Cleaning fluid	F1	F2	F3	F4	F5	F6	F7	F8	F9	F10	F11	F12	F13	F14	F15	F16	F17	F18	F19		F21	F22	F23	F24	F25
Lubricant	G1	G2	G3	G4	G5	G6	G7	G8	G9	G10	G11	G12	G13	G14	G15	G16	G17	G18		G20	G21	G22	G23	G24	G25
Petrol	H1	H2	H3	H4	H5	H6	H7	H8	H9	H10	H11	H12	H13	H14	H15	H16	H17		H19	H20	H21	H22	H23	H24	H25
Oil	I1	I2	I3	I4	I5	I6	I7	I8	I9	I10	I11	I12	I13	I14	I15	I16		I18	I19	I20	I21	I22	I23	I24	I25
Water	J1	J2	J3	J4	J5	J6	J7	J8	J9	J10	J11	J12	J13	J14	J15		J17	J18	J19	J20	J21	J22	J23	J24	J25
Tools — Lathe	K1	K2	K3	K4	K5	K6	K7	K8	K9	K10	K11	K12	K13	K14		K16	K17	K18	K19	K20	K21	K22	K23	K24	K25
Welding gear	L1	L2	L3	L4	L5	L6	L7	L8	L9	L10	L11	L12	L13		L15	L16	L17	L18	L19	L20	L21	L22	L23	L24	L25
Drill	M1	M2	M3	M4	M5	M6	M7	M8	M9	M10	M11	M12		M14	M15	M16	M17	M18	M19	M20	M21	M22	M23	M24	M25
Saw	N1	N2	N3	N4	N5	N6	N7	N8	N9	N10	N11		N13	N14	N15	N16	N17	N18	N19	N20	N21	N22	N23	N24	N25
Hammer	O1	O2	O3	O4	O5	O6	O7	O8	O9	O10		O12	O13	O14	O15	O16	O17	O18	O19	O20	O21	O22	O23	O24	O25
Places — WC	P1	P2	P3	P4	P5	P6	P7	P8	P9		P11	P12	P13	P14	P15	P16	P17	P18	P19	P20	P21	P22	P23	P24	P25
Office	Q1	Q2	Q3	Q4	Q5	Q6	Q7	Q8		Q10	Q11	Q12	Q13	Q14	Q15	Q16	Q17	Q18	Q19	Q20	Q21	Q22	Q23	Q24	Q25
Workshop	R1	R2	R3	R4	R5	R6	R7		R9	R10	R11	R12	R13	R14	R15	R16	R17	R18	R19	R20	R21	R22	R23	R24	R25
Warehouse	S1	S2	S3	S4	S5	S6		S8	S9	S10	S11	S12	S13	S14	S15	S16	S17	S18	S19	S20	S21	S22	S23	S24	S25
Canteen	T1	T2	T3	T4	T5		T7	T8	T9	T10	T11	T12	T13	T14	T15	T16	T17	T18	T19	T20	T21	T22	T23	T24	T25
People — Me	U1	U2	U3	U4		U6	U7	U8	U9	U10	U11	U12	U13	U14	U15	U16	U17	U18	U19	U20	U21	U22	U23	U24	U25
Classmate	V1	V2	V3		V5	V6	V7	V8	V9	V10	V11	V12	V13	V14	V15	V16	V17	V18	V19	V20	V21	V22	V23	V24	V25
My boss	W1	W2		W4	W5	W6	W7	W8	W9	W10	W11	W12	W13	W14	W15	W16	W17	W18	W19	W20	W21	W22	W23	W24	W25
The first aider	X1		X3	X4	X5	X6	X7	X8	X9	X10	X11	X12	X13	X14	X15	X16	X17	X18	X19	X20	X21	X22	X23	X24	X25
Teacher		Y2	Y3	Y4	Y5	Y6	Y7	Y8	Y9	Y10	Y11	Y12	Y13	Y14	Y15	Y16	Y17	Y18	Y19	Y20	Y21	Y22	Y23	Y24	Y25

Objective: To exchange information in order to solve a problem.

▶ **1** **Read, speak and solve a problem**

a Read the e-mail below to find out what the problem is.

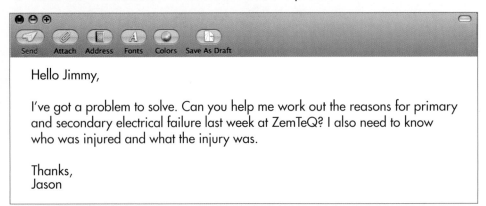

Hello Jimmy,

I've got a problem to solve. Can you help me work out the reasons for primary and secondary electrical failure last week at ZemTeQ? I also need to know who was injured and what the injury was.

Thanks,
Jason

Steve	*The warehouse electrical fire definitely involved incompetency. Poor old Harry.*
Sebastian	
Sammy	
Sidney	
Stephen	
Seb	
Samuel	
Seamus	
Stefan	
Shane	
Sid	
Scott	
Simon	
Sylvester	
Sandy	
Stanley	
Spencer	
Sam	
Seth	
Sean	
Stew	
Stuart	
Sven	
Stan	

b Choose a worker name opposite and then go to page 148 to find out what that person said. Copy only what the worker said onto the correct line next to each worker's name.

c Walk around the class exchanging information. Write the other workers' information.

d When you have all the information, work with a partner and complete the failure detail grid below. Use the answer grid to solve the puzzle.

Supervisors		1° Failure					1° Failure detail					2° Failure					2° Failure detail					Injury					Casualty				
		damaged insulation	poor work-systems	inadequate fuse	inadequate circuit-breaker	poor earthing	split sheaths	no permit to work	wrong rating	no cut-off	not inspected	incompetency	overheated apparatus	earth leak current	loose contacts	poor maintenance	untrained staff	loose connections	broken RCD	complacent work	bad record-keeping	minor burns	fatal shock	arc burn	low-voltage shock	major burns	Harry	Henny	Henry	Hugh	Howie
	Warehouse																														
	Workshop																														
	Plant																														
	Pipeline																														
	Tanks																														

Answer grid

Location	1° Failure	1° Failure detail	2° Failure	2° Failure detail	Injury	Casualty
Warehouse	Damage insulation					

Objective: To learn ways of saying why something happened and talking about the effects of it happening.

▶ **1** ⊙ **2:13 Listen and write**

Listen to the conversation and write the missing words and phrases below.

J Morning, Richard.

R Hello, Jimmy. What happened to your leg?

J I had an accident in my car on Monday. **1** _____ a tree, which led to this, a broken leg and me on crutches for six weeks.

R Ouch. That must have **2** _____. What caused **3** _____?

J Mainly, it was **4** _____ my cat.

R You're **5** _____.

J No, seriously, my cat made noises all night, so I didn't sleep. **6** _____ I overslept and **7** _____ me rushing in the morning ...

R Yes, **8** _____.

J Well, I took a **9** _____ to work, when suddenly an animal **10** _____ into the road, and led to me swerving and bang ... here I am. Want to buy a cat?

R **11** _____ cats, Jimmy. Never mind. Let me take your book while you **12** _____ what we did last week. Your turn to buy the coffee ... I think.

▶ **2** **Find and choose**

Write 1–12 next to the words and phrases that have a similar meaning to those from the conversation. Use some numbers more than once.

a	I crashed into	____	**k**	led to	____
b	carry on	____	**l**	ended up with	____
c	because of	____	**m**	joking	____
d	so	____	**n**	ran	____
e	been painful	____	**o**	run through	____
f	recap	____	**p**	down to	____
g	having me on	____	**q**	I hate	____
h	I loathe	____	**r**	leapt	____
i	sprang	____	**s**	quicker way	____
j	keep going	____			

▶ **3** **Read and speak**

With a partner, act out the conversation several times using different words and phrases from Task 2.

▶ **4** **Read and write**

a Read the scenarios opposite and choose one.

b With a partner, write out the conversation using words and phrases from Tasks 1 and 2.

c Practise your conversation and then perform it for the class.

A health and safety inspector gives a list of changes needed and explains what will happen if the changes are not made.

There have been five accidents recently in your section. Two friends discuss the reasons for the accidents and the damage and injuries resulting from them.

You and a friend are moaning about some of the rules in your section. You chat about some of the changes you would make if you were the boss and the effects your changes would have.

There has been a fatal injury with a man falling from a ladder. Over tea, two co-workers discuss why it happened and what changes will now happen in ladder use.

The English teacher is talking to a student about ways to improve his English and the effects of doing these things.

Activate your vocabulary
Go to page 152.

First aid and injury

1 Parts of the body

Objective: To learn parts of the human body.

▶ 1 Look and write

Work with a partner. Find 40 body parts in the wordsearch and use the words to label the body parts in the pictures.

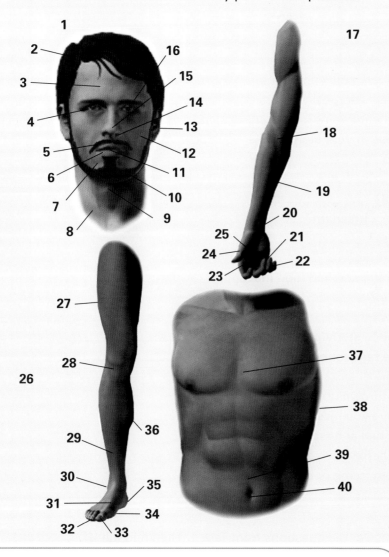

Q	T	H	E	A	D	H	E	E	L
R	A	H	B	U	T	H	U	M	B
C	E	E	R	C	H	I	N	E	J
H	G	L	Y	O	N	S	L	L	T
A	R	M	B	E	A	O	Z	S	M
P	R	B	D	O	S	T	E	R	N
N	A	V	A	L	W	H	A	X	O
W	K	L	U	P	C	E	R	K	F
B	B	R	M	Y	R	O	C	W	C
N	P	A	J	O	W	E	J	R	V
E	C	G	F	M	N	T	F	I	Y
S	H	I	N	K	E	O	I	S	Y
L	C	H	E	E	K	E	N	T	E
I	N	M	H	O	N	N	G	Z	S
P	D	I	A	C	O	A	E	T	P
S	D	S	N	A	S	I	R	O	S
W	M	U	D	L	T	L	N	E	T
B	D	O	M	F	R	I	A	I	O
K	A	L	U	F	I	J	I	J	M
Q	S	C	N	S	L	A	L	M	A
L	G	R	K	O	T	E	G	O	C
B	E	A	R	D	S	A	U	U	H
X	L	E	G	T	U	E	C	T	K
H	Z	E	A	R	U	O	G	H	N
X	A	E	Y	E	B	R	O	W	E
Y	G	I	F	I	N	G	E	R	E
D	W	B	R	G	T	H	I	G	H
F	F	F	O	O	T	U	E	M	A
S	Q	R	D	T	A	N	K	L	E
Z	F	O	R	E	H	E	A	D	P

▶ 2 Body mapping

Draw an outline of your body and follow the instructions below.

a Mark on your picture:
  1 cuts and bruises
  2 aches and pains
  3 illness and breaks

b Explain the markings on your body map to a partner.
c Discuss the causes of, and how to prevent these injuries and illnesses.
d Some students can present their body maps to the class for discussion.

▶ 3 Check what you remember

Work with a partner. Take it in turns to touch parts of your body. Your partner names the body part.

An A–Z of aches and pains

Objective: To learn vocabulary related to health problems and injuries, and to ask and answer questions about the same.

▶ 1   Spell the words

The jumbled words in these questions are in alphabetical order. So the jumbled word in sentence a begins with *a* and so on. Unscramble the words. Match some of the words to the pictures below and opposite.

a   Do you have an **gerally** to nuts or other foods? _____

b   How do you stop a cut from **lingebed**? _____

c   What does **stech** pain on the right side mean? _____

d   What makes you **zidyz** or faint? _____

e   Have you had an **celciter** shock from a machine? _____

f   How do you get **borfittes** in very cold conditions? _____

g   What's the difference between a **zrage** and a cut? _____

h   What gives you a **edeachha** or migraine? _____

i   What food causes **tingideneso** in your stomach? _____

j   Where is your **waj**? _____

k   What does a **keyind** do? _____

l   Have you ever broken a **mibl**? _____

m   Have you ever suffered from a **irgienam**? _____

n   How do you stop a **blondeese**? _____

o   How often do you work **meetrivo**? _____

p   Have you ever eaten something and had food **inoosping**? _____

q   What is **uniquen** used to treat? _____

r   What is the **verycore** position? _____

s   How do you take small wooden **sternlips** out of your finger? _____

t   What should a **remmotthere** read for body temperature? _____

u   When did you last feel **nullew** or sick? _____

v   When have you **timdove** or thrown up? _____

w   What **dunsow** or injuries have you received at work? _____

x   How many **X-sary** have you had at hospital? _____

y   Is **welloy** fever a problem where you live? _____

z   Have you ever used a **miZrem** frame or crutches? _____

▶ 2   Discuss

Work with a partner. Ask and answer the questions from Task 1. Then find out about other students in the class.

Objective: To learn how to talk about the cause and treatment of various injuries.

▶ 1 Look and match

Match these injuries with people in the picture.

1 dislocated shoulder ____		**11** backache ____
2 face rash ____		**12** broken leg ____
3 swollen foot ____		**13** skin burns ____
4 rodent bite ____		**14** bruised leg ____
5 bleeding nose ____		**15** broken tooth ____
6 sprained ankle ____		**16** bee sting ____
7 upset stomach ____		**17** gashed knee ____
8 fractured wrist ____		**18** arc eye ____
9 lacerated scalp ____		**19** pulled leg muscle ____
10 chest pain ____		**20** cut hand ____

▶ 2 Talk and write

Look at the table below. Discuss each of the 20 injuries with a partner and complete the table in note form as in the example.

Injury	Cause of injury	Treatment of injury	Length of absence
Dislocated shoulder	Fall from ladder	Joint to be put back in place Medicine given to relieve pain	2–3 weeks

▶ 3 Ask and answer

Ask your teacher about injuries he or she has had and how the injury was treated. Then ask other students.

4 ABC of first aid lecture

Objective: To listen to a lecture about giving first aid.

▶ 1 ⊛ 2:14 Listen and decide

Listen to the first part of the lecture and mark these statements true (T) or false (F).

a The lecture will fully prepare you to give first aid. _____

b The lecturer tells you what is most important in an emergency. _____

▶ 2 ⊛ 2:15 Listen and write

Listen again and write the missing words and phrases.

Hello guys, it's me again. We are here today to think about basic first aid to help people with serious injuries. Do you know where the 1 _____ is? Do you know who the 2 _____ is in your section? What do you do in an 3 _____? The important thing to say is you must do some 4 _____. What I will tell you will not equip you to deal with the situation, I will just explain a little about what you need to think about. So go and get that training. If you find someone in an emergency situation, the four priorities are:

1 check the situation – do not put yourself in 5 _____;

2 make the area 6 _____;

3 look after 7 _____ people first;

4 send for 8 _____.

Then attend the injured person – check for a 9 _____. Gently shake the shoulder and ask loudly 'Are you all right?'. If there is no response:

1 shout for help;

2 10 _____ the airway;

3 check for normal 11 _____;

4 take the 12 _____.

▶ 3 Ask and answer

Ask and answer these questions with a partner.

a What first aid do you know?

b What does your first-aid box contain?

c Who is your first-aider?

d Have you had first-aid training?

e Have you had to deal with a medical emergency?

▶ 4 ⊛ 2:16 Listen and choose

Listen to the next part of the lecture. Tick the statement below that is true.

a The lecturer implies that giving first aid is simple. ☐

b The lecturer implies that giving first aid is complicated. ☐

▶ 5 ⊛ 2:17 Listen and write

Listen again and write in the missing words and phrases.

Think of it as ABC.

A is for airway. Open the airway.

a Put your hand on his 1 _____.

b 2 _____ his head back gently.

c 3 _____ chin with two fingers.

B is for breathing. You know. Look, listen and feel for 4 _____ breath. If breathing is OK, put in recovery position. Plus, get help. If not breathing normally, a trained CPR person is needed.

C is for CPR – cardiopulmonary resuscitation. Cardio refers to 5 _____, pulmonary to 6 _____ and breathing and resuscitation to 7 _____. You want them to start breathing and their heart to start 8 _____ again.

So, you 9 _____ on their chest and help them to start breathing. I won't say more, you must get training to do CPR properly. But do it! You could 10 _____ somebody's life – at work, in the street, even at home.

▶ 6 Ask and answer

Answer these questions as a class.

a What's your normal breathing rate per minute?

b What's your pulse or heart rate?

c Have you seen or tried CPR?

5 | First-aid box

Objective: To learn how to talk about the typical contents of a first-aid box.

The contents of a first-aid box vary, depending on the company and the country the company is in. However, there are usually consistencies, e.g., medicine and painkillers are not usually kept in a first-aid box.

▶ 1 Listen and write

Work in groups of four. Student A turn to page 148 and read out the items 1–26 slowly and clearly. Students B, C and D listen and write down the items on the list.

1 _____ __	10 _____ __	19 _____ __
2 _____ __	11 _____ __	20 _____ __
3 _____ __	12 _____ __	21 _____ __
4 _____ __	13 _____ __	22 _____ __
5 _____ __	14 _____ __	23 _____ __
6 _____ __	15 _____ __	24 _____ __
7 _____ __	16 _____ __	25 _____ __
8 _____ __	17 _____ __	26 _____ __
9 _____ __	18 _____ __	

▶ 2 Look and match

Work with a partner. Match the items on your list with the pictures.

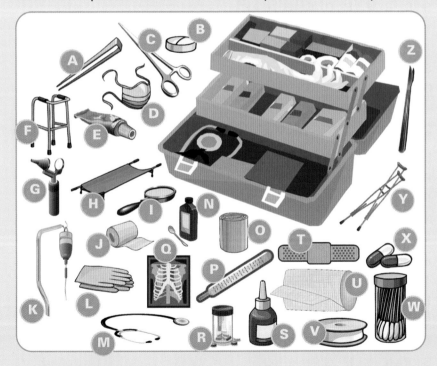

▶ 3 Discuss and list

Work again in your group of four. Look at the situations below and decide on the five items from the first-aid box that you would most need for each. Be prepared to explain your answers to the class.

1 In the workshop   2 In your home   3 On holiday   4 After an earthquake

Damaged goods

Objective: To learn the names of typical items around the workplace and talk about how each could be damaged.

▶ 1 Look and find

Work with a partner. Find 18 words or phrases in wordsearch A that describe damage. Then find 15 materials or typical items around the workplace in wordsearch B. Think about how the words in A could describe the items in B. Some of the words in B can be used more than once.

Example: *scratched glass*

A

A	Q	E	G	F	R	I	P	P	E	D	V	Z	T	D	X
C	R	A	C	K	E	D	I	C	P	J	I	N	E	W	M
B	R	O	K	E	N	F	R	I	Q	E	R	T	S	A	J
S	F	V	T	R	B	E	K	L	A	U	N	B	P	T	Z
L	R	T	W	J	J	N	S	E	B	E	M	P	L	E	C
E	S	D	I	T	A	T	W	W	D	K	D	W	I	R	B
A	O	K	S	O	C	X	S	Q	A	E	K	X	T	D	E
K	A	O	T	R	X	R	G	C	G	W	M	W	U	A	N
I	K	H	E	N	O	S	U	A	R	B	E	P	D	M	T
N	E	V	D	M	M	N	M	S	U	A	L	Q	D	A	N
G	D	S	O	H	G	A	B	X	H	E	T	A	N	G	J
P	O	M	G	W	D	P	B	D	R	E	E	C	C	E	I
O	Y	L	D	E	A	P	Y	P	Q	Q	D	R	H	D	V
R	S	P	R	T	A	E	A	V	Y	Q	C	B	O	E	K
E	B	I	H	O	A	D	S	T	A	I	N	E	D	A	D
D	F	Z	Y	D	Y	P	D	W	E	G	G	R	Y	Y	S

B

B	N	E	E	D	U	F	N	G	T	R	P	L	U	G	T
U	T	R	X	W	T	L	R	H	L	I	N	R	O	G	R
L	J	E	T	H	U	U	R	E	H	A	W	A	O	O	R
B	P	O	I	O	M	D	B	Q	P	F	S	P	L	G	A
N	V	E	N	O	X	J	N	E	R	O	L	S	Q	G	G
U	Q	D	G	X	G	S	N	S	A	E	R	C	W	L	W
X	R	M	U	D	Q	X	A	P	B	V	O	T	U	E	B
K	K	T	I	X	C	Z	I	I	Y	R	W	G	S	S	E
A	A	V	S	M	J	W	L	T	N	R	K	O	B	N	J
U	I	M	H	K	U	D	S	Y	G	R	B	G	O	H	M
M	D	E	E	K	R	U	L	L	E	Q	E	V	R	D	U
U	T	D	R	E	A	T	S	P	N	Y	M	G	I	L	Q
I	C	B	V	M	A	X	A	I	U	G	L	O	V	E	A
W	O	O	D	O	I	P	T	O	K	T	Y	Y	Z	E	R
W	I	R	E	D	G	M	V	D	Y	Q	D	X	C	T	V
D	Q	I	N	F	D	O	E	U	D	U	S	T	E	R	B

1 _____
2 _____
3 _____
4 _____
5 _____
6 _____
7 _____
8 _____
9 _____
10 _____
11 _____
12 _____
13 _____
14 _____
15 _____
16 _____
17 _____
18 _____

▶ 2 Look and match

Look at the workers in the picture below and the items they are holding. Match words from the two wordsearches to describe each item and write sentences in your notebook.

Example: *Worker C is holding a broken bulb.*

▶ 3 Read and solve

Find out the name of each worker by reading the text beneath the picture.

Ted needed to put a fire out. On his left, Stan was in the dark. Bob always had a company shirt. Jim couldn't stick any wood together. Gary was angry that a pipe was damaged. Tony had to replace a windowpane. Den used his hand PPE to put out a blaze. Ken lost his incident details. Rob had to wash his cleaning cloth. Tom wanted to know who had sat on his nail container. John needs some new PPE eyewear. Tim left his planks out in the rain and Rory dropped his timber off the lorry. Larry doesn't know what he will hammer into his MDF sheet. Steve isn't happy that he can't wipe the dust from his desk. Darren was unsure how to conduct electricity from the fuse box. Len dropped his report in the sink and Dean is worried about protecting his hands when handling.

▶ 4 Tell your own story

Try to remember any damaged items you have seen in your workplace recently. Tell a partner how you think they were damaged.

Objective: To learn informal ways of talking about procedures and processes.

In both office and workshop environments, there are standard operating procedures (SOPs) to follow.

▶ 1 ⊚ 2:18 Listen and write

Listen to the conversation and write the missing words and phrases below.

J Hello, Richard. **1** _____?

R Fine, just fine. Well, there is one small thing. How do I **2** _____ a parking permit?

J Phew ... Do you have any good friends in Admin?

R No, I don't.

J Bad luck. Well **3** _____ go up to Level 3 and get a form. Fill it in, **4** _____ go to services and get a signature.

R **5** _____?

J No, no. Next, **6** _____ to Level 3 and get a request form. Again, fill it in and then, **7** _____, you get your line manager to sign it and **8** _____ to Level 3.

R Wow ... maybe it is easier to get the bus or a lift from someone.

J Oh, it's not so bad. It will take **9** _____ days, **10** _____. That's nothing. My friend just got a new ID badge. It took nine weeks! Anyway, **11** _____.

R Thanks, Jimmy. I owe you. **12** _____, you don't drive past my house on your way do you?

▶ 2 Find and choose

Write 1–12 next to the words and phrases that have a similar meaning to those from the conversation. Use some numbers more than once.

a	how's it going	___	**l**	how are you keeping	___
b	return it	___	**m**	post it back	___
c	incidentally	___	**n**	pick up	___
d	all right	___	**o**	that's all	___
e	a few	___	**p**	when that's done	___
f	first of all	___	**q**	two or three	___
g	after that	___	**r**	last of all	___
h	get hold of	___	**s**	how's life	___
i	lastly	___	**t**	fingers crossed	___
j	at most	___	**u**	to start with	___
k	return	___	**v**	as simple as that	___

▶ 3 Read and speak

With a partner, act out the conversation several times using different words and phrases from Task 2.

▶ 4 Read and write

a Read the scenarios opposite and choose one.
b With a partner, write out the conversation using words and phrases from Tasks 1 and 2.
c Practise your conversation and then perform it for the class.

A worker in your company explains to a school-leaver how to go about getting a job in your company and all the steps involved.

A site manager for a construction company is describing the process of house building to a group of workers on site. They have questions for him and politely interrupt him occasionally.

A workshop manager describes the main stages of a job in the workshop to a new recruit on his first day.

Your car breaks down in the middle of nowhere. You call the rescue service and they give you step-by-step instructions of what to check on your car.

You are explaining to your teacher the main production stages of your company's primary product or service.

Activate your vocabulary
Go to page 152.

Incident reports

1 Writing an incident report

Objective: To learn the key elements of an incident report and focus on the key words and phrases used in incident reports.

▶ 1 Read and think

Jimmy has received a lot of advice about how to write an incident report. Read the reports below and think about the key words and phrases that are missing.

'Remember, when you write a 1 _____ a 2 _____, you must give to the reader. Make it 3 _____. It must be easy for the 4 _____ to understand.'

'A 5 _____ is important to sum up and give a clear idea of the 6 _____ of the incident.'

'The cause tells us what the 7 _____ is for the 8 _____, or what it 9 _____.'

'The 10 _____ of the incident or 11 _____ need to be detailed, saying what injuries or 12 _____ was done.'

'Key questions to ask are:
13 _____ – explaining exactly what happened;
14 _____ – giving the time and date;
15 _____ – identifying the exact location;
16 _____ – pinpointing the people involved; and
17 _____ – describing how it came to happen.'

'Report not only accidents and incidents, but also any 18 _____ es.'

'Make sure you talk to as many 19 _____ as possible to get their statements.'

'Find out if correct 20 _____ were followed, if people were properly 21 _____, and if an 22 _____ would have found the problem before the incident happened.'

'23 _____ to see if it has happened before – were the lessons learnt?'

'Get 25 _____ s for your report: you, the manager, witnesses and victims – get them all!'

'Reporting even minor near misses can help 24 _____ serious accidents in the future.'

▶ 2 Look and write

Work with a partner. Find words and phrases in the wordsearch and use them to complete the incident reports in Task 1.

D	H	O	W	L	W	H	E	R	E	I	B	V	S	I	M
R	E	S	U	L	T	E	D	F	R	O	M	E	T	N	H
X	G	R	E	A	D	E	R	G	R	E	T	A	X	S	A
A	D	A	M	A	G	E	W	J	R	A	E	C	M	P	I
M	O	H	I	A	K	R	M	U	G	J	P	C	E	E	N
C	A	U	S	E	A	Q	T	I	D	R	I	I	S	C	C
E	W	H	O	E	I	A	T	T	Z	M	S	D	S	T	I
F	W	V	L	T	N	S	M	T	R	S	T	E	A	I	D
F	I	C	R	G	E	C	N	W	M	A	Q	N	G	O	E
E	T	C	I	V	V	E	T	C	H	F	I	T	E	N	N
C	N	S	N	A	V	D	T	W	O	Q	G	N	R	O	T
T	E	I	N	E	A	R	M	I	S	S	U	H	E	Z	Y
S	S	P	R	D	G	R	E	A	S	O	N	E	X	D	T
S	S	P	F	S	C	O	N	C	L	U	S	I	O	N	H
S	B	G	B	C	J	R	R	E	P	O	R	T	J	T	J
W	O	R	K	S	Y	S	T	E	M	S	X	W	H	E	N

▶ 3 Ask and answer

Ask and answer these questions about incidents in small groups.

1 Have you ever written an incident or accident report?
2 What is the difference between an incident and an accident report?
3 What documents need your personal signature on them?
4 Have you ever witnessed an accident?
5 How do reports prevent accidents from happening in the future?
6 Whose responsibility is it to investigate incidents in your section?

2 | Incident forms lecture

Objective: To listen to detailed information about completing an incident report.

▶ 1   Read and think

Look carefully at the incident report opposite. Guess some of the terms and headings that are missing.

▶ 2   ◉ 2:19 Listen and answer

Listen to Richard's lecture and answer these questions.

a What do we hope to learn from an incident report? _____

b Who writes the conclusions? _____

c What changes at ZemTeQ every week? _____

▶ 3   ◉ 2:20 Listen and write

Listen again and fill in the missing terms (A–L) on the report opposite.

▶ 4   Forming questions

Here are some questions that the investigator will want answered, but the words are in the wrong order. Write the questions in the correct order.

1 who people were involved the? _____

2 the worker was injured who? _____

3 accident caused what the? _____

4 incident what from effects resulted the? _____

5 did happen the how incident? _____

6 place did take where the incident? _____

7 occur when did incident the? _____

8 were made recommendations what? _____

▶ 5   Ask and answer

Ask and answer the questions in Task 4 for the incident report opposite.

1 _____

2 _____

3 _____

4 _____

5 _____

6 _____

7 _____

8 _____

▶ 6   Walk and talk

Think of an incident that has occurred in your workplace and answer the questions in Task 4. Walk around the class asking people about incidents in their workplaces.

ZemTeQ *IF 62F*		**INCIDENT FORM**	

A		*Justin Lee 4215N*	C		*11:30 a.m. 13/03/2008*
B		*Warehouse Picker/Packer*	D		*Warehouse D – area G17*
Department		*Shipping & Storage*	Injury type		*broken left arm, cuts/bruises*
Report by		*Jules Nut*	Estimated Absence		*4/5 weeks*
Position/Dept.		*Supervisor/Warehousing*			

E *give brief details of incident*

The incident with Mr Justin Lee, a warehouse picker/packer happened at 11:30 a.m. on 13th March 2008 in warehouse D, area G17. The operative needed to access the top level of shelving to get an item for shipping. There were no forklifts in the area, so he called the supervisor Mr Brown to send one. None came in the next 15 minutes. The operative climbed the shelving to the top without a harness or assistance. He slipped on some loose items and fell 5 m to the floor. He stayed there unconscious until found by Mr Green 10 minutes later. Mr Green called for an ambulance and then gave Mr Lee first aid and care. Mr Lee was taken to hospital at 11:50 a.m. by ambulance. He has a broken left arm and minor cuts and bruises. He is expected to be absent for 4–5 weeks.

F

G			H		
1	No permit		1	Inadequate guard	
2	Failure to warn		2	Inadequate PPE	
3	Failure to secure	✓	3	Defective tools/equipment	
4	Safety devices off		4	Restricted space	
5	Removed safety devices	✓	5	Noise exposure	
6	Wrong use of equipment		6	Fire hazards	
7	Incorrect PPE	✓	7	Poor housekeeping	
8	Incorrect loading		8	Gas/fume/dust/vapour	
9	Incorrect placement		9	Radiation exposure	
10	Incorrect handling	✓	10	Extreme temperature	
11	Incorrect task position		11	Inadequate lighting	
12	Horseplay		12	Inadequate ventilation	

I

1	Contact with machinery or material being machined		9	Drowning or asphyxiation	
2	Hit by moving, flying or falling object		10	Exposure to or contact with harmful substance	
3	Hit by moving vehicle		11	Exposure to fire	
4	Hit something fixed or stationary		12	Exposure to an explosion	
5	Injured handling, lifting or carrying		13	Contact with electricity	
6	Slip, trip or fall on same level		14	Violence	
7	Fall from height	✓	15	Injured by animal	
8	Trapped by something collapsing				

J *make any recommendations to prevent future incidents*

Mr Lee should not have climbed the shelving to get the item without a harness or assistance and should have waited for a forklift to help. Further training and meetings should highlight this in the future.

K

Mr Tim Brown – 6571D – Shipping and Storage Supervisor
Mr Ahmed Green – 19041D – Shipping and Storage Supervisor

L ....: ~~signature~~ ....

Date: *15th March 2008*

Objective: To practise writing an accident report and to amend an accident report.

▶ 1 Look and think

Work with a partner. The pictures below tell the story of an accident at work. Try to put the pictures into a logical order and make a list of key words and phrases that you would need to tell the story.

▶ 2 Look and match

Work with the same partner. Match these words and phrases with what you can
see in the pictures and think about how they can help you to tell the story.

entanglement bad practice choking conveyor belt **plug** unconscious
BOXES cable monitor **packing machine** drip
bed stretcher bottle ambulance doctor cleaning fluid
out-cold TRIP hospital bed
patient notes hot parts socket RAISE-THE-ALARM HEADPHONES leak
alarm clock polisher **control-panel** paramedic spill

▶ 3 Write a report

Work with the same partner. Use the words to write a report of what you think
happened. Read your report to the class and then, as a class, decide which is
the best and most probable account.

Incident details

_____
_____
_____
_____
_____
_____
_____
_____
_____
_____
_____

▶ 4 Amend a report

Your teacher will give you a copy of the actual report that Jimmy wrote. Remember
that Jimmy is a trainee, so his report is not perfect. It contains some unnecessary
information. With a partner, decide what to take out so that the report is shorter,
clearer and easier to understand.

Objective: To read information and solve a puzzle.

▶ 1   Read and match

Read the sentences and decide which report (1–11) they refer to.

a The injured man was cold and was being sick.   ____

b The body was discovered without a head.   ____

c The man had injured hands and ears.   ____

d A number of sporty men were injured.   ____

e The injured men were not looking at each other.   ____

f The injured man had sports shoes on.   ____

g The injured man's clothing was dirty.   ____

h The injured man didn't know what had happened.   ____

i The victim had injured his eye.   ____

j The injured man had been reading and drinking tea or coffee.   ____

k The dead man was dressed to go swimming.   ____

1 A man was found lying in a car park with a flagpole. He was unconscious and was wearing trainers. There is a dead bird next to him. His hands are black. It is midday and his clothes are wet.

2 A man was lying unconscious in a storeroom, with a hat and gloves on. There was a puddle of water around him and a lot of light was coming in through the open door. The door had a sign that said 'Keep Shut'. He had a bruised forehead, bruised palms and blood coming out of his ears.

3 A man had a bleeding eye. He worked with the lathes in Workshop 4. He was new to this job, but there should not have been any problems as he had many years' experience in other areas. There are clear safety signs around the lathe.

4 There was a factory fire that resulted in the work area being charred and burnt. The fire started on top of the building. Afterwards, a man wearing trunks and a snorkel was found dead.

5 A headless body was found in the lumberyard. There was a lot of cut timber around in same-size planks. A chainsaw was running very loudly on the ground. The dead worker had red spots on his hands. It was 3.20 p.m. and the man's lunchbox was open with jam sandwiches uneaten inside it.

6 There was a ventilator in the wall with a dead bird on it. Three men were unconscious around cylinders on the floor. There was a wheelbarrow on the floor and unused welding equipment. The men all played football last night for ZemTeq United, when they lost a big match against another company's team.

7 A man was sat on the floor holding his back and rubbing his head. He didn't remember anything. There was a sack truck nearby and a large damaged box on the floor with a cat on top of it. A door was open to his left and there was a high shelving rack to his right with boxes on the top shelf.

8 A man was found under chemical storage tanks. He was lying on the floor unconscious. It was a very hot day, his sweaty body was found next to an open flask and a newspaper. Around midday, he was discovered by friends with small puddles seeping into the sand around him.

9 It was Tuesday, the day after payday. A man was by a table in the canteen at lunchtime, shivering, sweating and vomiting. He had bags under his eyes. He had a sandwich on the floor next to him and had spilt a cup of coffee. His hands were red. He worked in the kitchens.

10 A man with a ripped tie was unconscious in an ambulance. He had a ruler in his hand that he always carried because of his job. He was found after the tea break in the packing room. He had grease on the front of his shirt with a bad cut on his head and a bleeding nose. It was a beautiful day outside.

11 The incident happened outside a new building site in the delivery area for bricks. It was raining very hard. There were two vehicles, a digger and a forklift, both damaged and smoking. They were both facing in opposite directions. Two radio stations were playing very loudly at the time. Both drivers suffered bad injuries to their backs and faces.

▶ 2   Read and think

Work in small groups. Read Reports 1 and 2. Try to come up with a sequence of events to explain what happened. The teacher will give you a possible version afterwards.

▶ 3   Read, think and explain

Do the same with Reports 3–11. When you have explanations for each incident, present them to the whole class. As a class, decide the best explanation for each incident.

5 | E-mail tennis

Objective: To practise reading and writing e-mails.

▶ 1 Think and plan

Think of an incident at work you were involved in or remember well. You are going to be a witness to that incident, so make sure you can answer the questions from the incident form in Lesson 2 (page 117).

You will e-mail answers to an investigator's questions. You will then swap roles and act as the investigator. Ask about your partner's incident in a separate series of e-mails.

▶ 2 Write and swap

Work with a partner. Write the e-mails according to the instruction boxes. Exchange sheets after each e-mail so that two complete sets of e-mails are written.

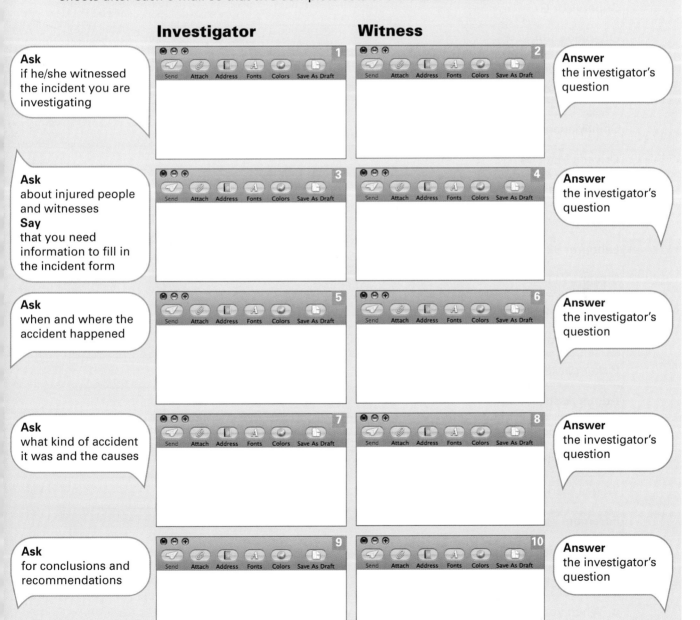

Investigator

Witness

Ask
if he/she witnessed the incident you are investigating

Answer
the investigator's question

Ask
about injured people and witnesses
Say
that you need information to fill in the incident form

Answer
the investigator's question

Ask
when and where the accident happened

Answer
the investigator's question

Ask
what kind of accident it was and the causes

Answer
the investigator's question

Ask
for conclusions and recommendations

Answer
the investigator's question

ZemTeQ incident puzzle

Objective: To exchange information in order to solve a problem.

▶ 1 **Read, speak and solve a problem**

Jimmy has been asked to find out about five incidents that all happened at ZemTeQ last week. He must find out: what happened, where, what time, who was involved, the injury that resulted and what caused it to happen. To do this, he must first get all the information by talking to the witnesses below and writing down their statements.

a Choose a witness name below and then go to page 149 to find out what that witness said. Copy only what your person said into the correct line below.

Driver 1	*The incident with Hans happened at 20 past 4, an hour before Harry's incident.*
Supervisor G	
Operative 17A	
Deputy Supervisor C4	
Machine Operator G91	
Shift Manager 3	
Driver's Mate D4	
General Manager	
CEO	
Labourer 92	
Cleaner Y11	
Chief Engineer	
Quality Inspector 9	
Picker/packer	
Admin Assistant 82	
Assistant Manager 4	
Electrician 16	
Wages Clerk 9	
Foreman	
Catering Assistant 12	

b Walk around the class exchanging the other witnesses' information.

c When you have all the information, work with a partner and complete the table above. Use the answer grid opposite to solve the puzzle.

Worker	Accident					Time					Location					Injury					Cause				
	Handling chemicals	Forklift	Fall on stairs	Electric shock	Lathe	04:05	4:20 p.m.	20:05	5:20 p.m.	05:05	Block U	Block O	Block I	Block E	Block A	Back	Cut hand	Broken arm	Vomit and burns	Unconscious and burns	Incorrect PPE	No guard	Spillage	Poor housekeeping	No signal
Hans						✗	✓	✗	✗	✗															
Harry						✗	✗	✗	✓	✗															
Harold							✗		✗																
Henny							✗		✗																
Henry							✗		✗																

▶ 2 Read and order

Put these sentences from Jimmy's incident report in the correct order.

a Then he picked up the sulphuric acid from the lab at 4 a.m. on the night shift on Wednesday 24th. _____

b The supervisor called for assistance and an ambulance. _____

c The supervisor told him to use gloves, overalls and a face mask for the job, which he ignored. _____

d Henry O'Rourke was told to take a bottle of sulphuric acid from the labs to the storeroom. _____

e Following that, he gave first aid and an ambulance arrived to take Henry to hospital. _____

f Next, he carried the hazardous substance down the corridor and put it on a table. _____

g Henry was found on the floor, vomiting with burns to his skin. _____

h He started to feel a little faint and his skin was itching. _____

i First, he got his supervisor to sign the permit to work. _____

j He called his supervisor at 4:05 a.m., who arrived two minutes later. _____

▶ 3 Write a report

Work with a partner. Choose one of the other accidents from the puzzle and write a report. Add details of what you think might have happened. Read your report to the class.

Objective: To learn informal expressions for describing things.

▶ **1** 🎧 **2:21 Listen and write**

Listen to the conversation and write the missing words and phrases below.

J Hello, Richard. You look worried. 1 _____?

R Oh, hello, Jimmy. Yes, I am. I have lost my bag. It has some large cheques in it and my wallet.

J OK, 2 _____. 3 _____?

R Well, it's a bag ... er ... a briefcase, with a handle and my name on it.

J 4 _____. 5 _____?

R Well ... it's 6 _____. About 80 by 50.

J And what colour is it?

R It's black, with a gold security lock. And a black handle.

J 7 _____?

R Brand new. I bought it last week.

J And what's it made of?

R It's made of very expensive leather.

J 8 _____, you need to go to lost property and talk to Sammy. He will 9 _____. I'll look around here.

R 10 _____, Jimmy. Er ... what does Sammy look like?

J Well, he's very tall and ...

▶ **2** **Find and choose**

Write 1–10 next to the words and phrases that have a similar meaning to those from the conversation. Use some numbers more than once.

a what's wrong	____	**i** what's up	____
b thanks very much	____	**j** thanks	____
c sort this out	____	**k** pretty big	____
d is it new	____	**l** OK	____
e calm down	____	**m** everything OK	____
f is it old	____	**n** how big is it	____
g well	____	**o** relax	____
h can you describe it	____	**p** right	____

▶ **3** **Read and speak**

With a partner, act out the conversation several times using different words and phrases from Task 2.

▶ **4** **Read and write**

a Read the scenarios opposite and choose one.

b With a partner, write out the conversation using words and phrases from Tasks 1 and 2.

c Practise your conversation and then perform it for the class.

Your house has just been robbed and you saw the burglars leaving. You are describing them and the items they stole to the police.

You are a tourist on vacation and start chatting to a tourist from another city in your country. Each of you describes your hometown and the people from that area.

A worker is talking to a trainee and asking him to fetch a particular drill that is needed. There are hundreds of drills in the storeroom, so a good description is needed by the trainee.

Two workers are discussing their company sites. Both give accounts of an aerial view of their company and its different sections and buildings.

Some students have invited the teacher to a dinner at one of their houses. There are no house numbers and so they have to describe what the house looks like.

Activate your vocabulary
Go to page 152.

Other hazards

1 | Hazards recap lecture

Objective: To listen to detailed information about completing an incident report.

In this lecture, Richard talks about the main hazards that you have seen. He also mentions two that you have not yet seen.

▶ 1 Look and match

Match the words in the box with the pictures.

> no right-turn   no smoking   no U-turn   noise   poison   pocketknife
> radiation   saw   scaffold   sharp object   alarm   battery   biological hazards
> bulb   fall   slips   extinguisher   falling objects   falling rocks   flammable
> speedometer   forklift   knife   ladder   low height   machine hazard
> no ladders   no pedestrians   switch   ear protection   trip   truck   wires
> socket   screwdriver

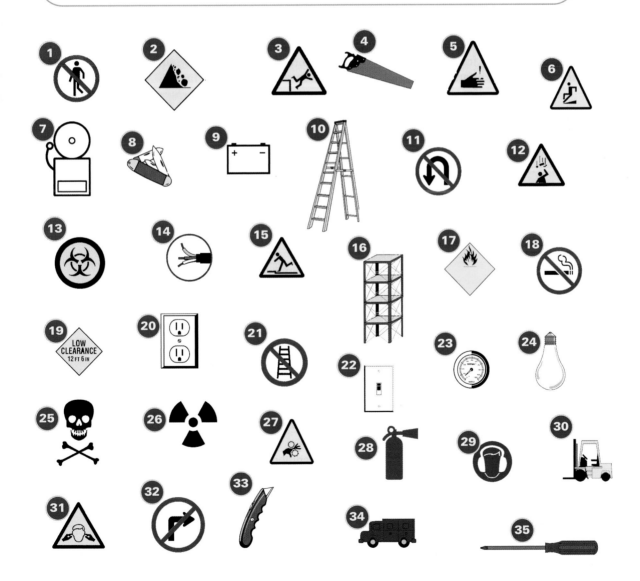

▶ 2   Revision

Talk with a partner. Try to remember as much as possible about the subjects below. Partners should talk briefly to the class about one of the subjects.

a PPE
b chemical safety
c incident reporting
d environmental safety
e first aid

f fire safety
g access safety
h machine/equipment safety
i handling safety
j construction

k risk assessment
l hand-held safety equipment
m electrical safety
n transport safety

▶ 3   ⊕ 2:22 Listen and write

Listen to Richard talk about eight of the subjects from Task 2. Write them in order.

1 _____
2 _____
3 _____
4 _____

5 _____
6 _____
7 _____
8 _____

▶ 4   ⊕ 2:23 Listen and match

Look at the list of words for a minute. Listen to the lecture introduction again and tick the words you hear. Then match each word to a subject from Task 3.

	Heard it?	Subject?
ergonomics		
working at height		
slips		
crushing		
cutting		
trains		
corrosive		
vehicles		
falling objects		
radiation		
impact		
pollution		
entrances		
burns		
fire types		
manual handling		
sack trucks		
lifting		
shock		

	Heard it?	Subject?
trips		
mechanical handling		
falls		
pedestrians		
excavations		
stabbing		
friction	✓	h
irritant		
shearing		
vibration		
signs		
noise		
flammable materials		
explosive		
extinguishers		
fuses		
biological hazards		
acids		
entanglement		

▶ 5   Class quiz

a Work in teams. Each team writes two questions about each of the eight subjects from the lecture.

b Teams then take it in turns to ask their questions to the other teams. The team with the highest score wins.

2 | Noise

Objective: To talk and read about the problem of noise.

Noise is part of our everyday work and home life. The problem is that loud noise can damage your hearing permanently. People who work in noisy environments often do not realize there is a problem until it is too late.

▶ 1 Odd-one-out

Work with a partner and sit back-to-back. Student A should look at the pictures below and Student B should look at the pictures on page 150. For each set of three, you must find a set name and identify the odd-one-out. At the end of the activity, check to see if you have circled the same picture for each set.

▶ 2 Think and talk

Noise is measured in decibels (dB). At ZemTeQ, anyone working with noise levels over 80 dB needs ear protection. There is a chart on page 150 that tells you how loud certain noises are. Work with a partner. See if you can add the noises in the box to the chart in the correct place.

▶ 3 Read and choose

Jimmy was asked to put some information on the ZemTeQ website about ear protection for employees. Complete the information using the words in the box.

> sound   reusable   wearer   glasses
> absorbs   reducing   two   effective
> reduction   fit   passed
> ear   defenders   disposable   problem
> comfortable   maintained   wear and tear

Ear protection

There are **1** _____ main types of ear protection: earplugs and ear **2** _____ (also called earmuffs). Earplugs are made of a material that **3** _____ sound. They should **4** _____ comfortably into the ear. There are **5** _____ types, which you can use several times, and **6** _____ types, which you throw away after you have used them. Both must fit well in the ear to be effective in **7** _____ noise for the **8** _____. The **9** _____ with earplugs is that they do not reduce sound **10** _____ through the bone of the **11** _____. Ear defenders reduce **12** _____ much better at all frequencies than earplugs. Normally, they are more **13** _____ to wear than earplugs, and they reduce the sound passed through the bone of the ear. However, they may be less **14** _____ if the wearer has long hair, wears **15** _____ or earrings. If you wear a face shield or helmet, the **16** _____ in sound can be less. They should be **17** _____ well and checked often to look for **18** _____.

Objective: To learn how to use superlative adjectives and to practise using them in the context of staff appraisal.

▶ 1 Think and write

Work with a partner. Richard and Jimmy are discussing some facts. First, help Jimmy complete the questions using a word from bubble A. Then choose one of Richard's answers from bubble B.

A

deepest   expensive   heaviest   **highest**
youngest **fastest** coldest **busiest**
hottest **deadliest** LONGEST
most DRIEST **wettest** poorest
strongest

B

Atacama Desert   King Cobra **Japan**
3 hr, 2 min, 04 sec   **K2**
J F Kennedy (43 yrs)   Uridium
Hawaii (58°C) Switzerland
South Pole (672 mph) NILE
Malawi ($600 GDP)
Lake Victoria   Blue whale
BEIJING AIRPORT
Vostok, Russia (-89°C)
Everest Kauai, Hawaii (360 days/yr)
Peregrine Falcon (200 mph)
Libya (58°C) box jellyfish
Mount Washington (372 mph)
Bangladesh (360 days/yr)
elephant Sergey Brin (Google)
Yemen ($900 GDP)
3.12 m Hank, California
Heathrow Airport Lake Baikal
North Pole (-89°C)
Colombian people   *Amazon*
cheetah (74 mph)
Sahara Desert

1   What is the _____ river in the world?
2   Where is the _____ place to live?
3   What is the _____ animal on Earth?
4   What is the _____ country in the world?
5   Which is the _____ desert in the world?
6   Where is the _____ place on Earth?
7   Where is the _____ wind on the planet?
8   Which is the _____ airport in the world?
9   What location is the _____ on Earth?
10 What is the _____ mountain on Earth?
11 Who was the _____ US president?
12 What is the _____ animal on the planet?
13 Where is the _____ place on Earth?
14 What is the _____ lake on Earth?
15 What is the _____ mammal on Earth?

▶ 2 Class quiz

With the same partner, write ten questions using ten different superlatives. Take it in turns to ask other students your questions. The winning partnership is the one with the most correct answers.

▶ 3 Read and choose

There are three trainee workers in the workshop, but because of cutbacks there is only one job. The personnel manager has asked people in the workshop about workers A, B and C. Read their statements on page 149 and use the table to rank each trainee 1st, 2nd or 3rd according to the qualities. 1st is the best and 3rd is the worst.

▶ 4 Talk and decide

Work in small groups. Discuss each of the trainees and decide who should get the job. Use superlative forms of the adjectives in the table.

Example: *Trainee A is the friendliest worker.*

4 | Vibration

> **Objective:** To read and talk about the problem of vibration and to learn some common acronyms, especially those related to vibration.

▶ 1 Find the acronyms

Work in teams. You have 15 minutes. You score a point for each acronym you can find in the wordsearch and another point if you know what it stands for. The team with the most points wins.

Example: *LED stands for light-emitting diode.*

K	W	C	A	H	V	B	M	I	L	I	O	U	U	N	G	L	H	M	B	A	W	W	F	J
P	G	F	M	S	E	F	L	E	A	R	S	I	N	Y	J	E	C	C	S	C	U	B	A	M
H	I	J	A	B	P	V	C	U	S	I	A	K	F	C	G	D	C	O	H	A	P	M	I	L
F	W	T	D	C	P	C	U	M	E	B	V	S	C	B	D	I	T	D	U	G	C	M	E	C
L	E	G	I	P	T	O	K	P	R	M	Y	A	N	B	P	R	V	M	M	S	V	D	D	D
C	P	R	Y	V	H	S	B	H	I	G	M	T	N	C	W	W	W	S	N	B	A	Q	C	F

▶ 2 Read, talk and choose

Work with a partner. Look at the picture and the acronyms relating to vibration injury. Tick the correct definition below.

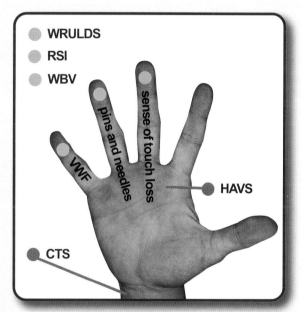

- WRULDS
- RSI
- WBV
- pins and needles
- sense of touch loss
- VWF
- HAVS
- CTS

1 RSI stands for:

   A really serious injury ☐

   B right side injury ☐

   C repetitive strain injury ☐

2 HAVS stands for:

   A hand and vein sickness ☐

   B hand arm vibration syndrome ☐

   C hurt arm vascular signs ☐

3 CTS stands for:

   A carpal tunnel syndrome ☐

   B cut thumb shakes ☐

   C can't think sickness ☐

4 VWF stands for:

   A vibration white finger ☐

   B very white finger ☐

   C very wide finger ☐

5 WBV stands for:

   A whole blood volume ☐

   B whole body volume ☐

   C whole body vibration ☐

6 WRULDS stands for:

   A was right under lighting daily sickness ☐

   B work-related upper limb disorders ☐

   C work right under little danger stress ☐

▶ 3 Read and complete

Jimmy has received an e-mail from a co-worker about vibration hazards and injuries. Use the acronyms from Task 2 to complete it.

○ ⊖ ⊕

Send   Attach   Address   Fonts   Colors   Save As Draft

Hi Jimmy,

Here's the info you asked for. **1** _____ are a group of illnesses that affect the neck, shoulders, arms, elbows, wrists, hands and fingers. For example, tenosynovitis affects the tendons and **2** _____ affects the tendons through the carpal bone in the hand specifically. Another term used to describe these is **3** _____, as the injuries are due to repetitive movement such as pulling, pushing, reaching, twisting or lifting. Factors affecting how serious it is include time, posture, vibrating tools and temperatures. Tools like drills, sanders and grinders create a lot of vibration that passes along the arm to the rest of the body.

4 _____ deals specifically with exposure of external **5** _____. A lot of workers had **6** _____ at ZemTeQ last year, with poor blood circulation in their hands. Most don't notice until they finish the shift. Some of their fingers went white. Also, some get **7** _____, which passes through the feet and affects the whole body. It is caused by vibrating machines. I think we need a new risk assessment for the whole company specifically targeted at vibration. It causes so many problems. Anyway, hope this helps.

Derek

▶ 4 Ask and answer

Work with a partner. Ask and answer these questions about your own job.

1 Do you use vibrating tools?
2 Do you stand near vibrating tools?
3 Do you get aches or pain in your hands, arms or neck? Do you know why?
4 Do you ever get pins and needles?
5 Do you get numbness in your hands sometimes?
6 Do you use tools for a long time or in difficult positions?

▶ 5 Take part in a meeting

In small groups, discuss vibration issues in your area using the agenda below. Feed back to the class on your discussion.

Section Meeting   Date: ▓▓▓▓▓▓▓

Vibration issues

1 What jobs involve possible WRULDS in your section?

2 What controls are already used to reduce risk due to vibration in your section?

3 What else can you do to control risks due to vibration in your section?

Objective: To read and talk about the role of ergonomics in improving the work environment for the worker.

Ergonomics is about the 'fit' between the worker and the work he/she does. It is about making sure that the job, the environment and the equipment are all suitable for the worker. Ergonomics lowers the potential for accidents, injury and ill health and improves performance and productivity.

▶ **1   Look and discuss**

The picture below shows one of the trainers at ZemTeQ in his classroom.
Work with a partner. Answer the questions in the two sections below.
Are the ergonomics of his job and workplace appropriate?

The workplace

a   Is the equipment appropriate for the job? Is it the right size and shape?

b   Is the room temperature right?

c   Is the humidity in the room suitable?

d   Is the lighting appropriate?

e   Is the noise level appropriate?

f   Is vibration a problem?

The worker

g   Is his height or weight a problem?

h   Is his fitness level right for the job?

i   Is his body strength acceptable for the job?

j   Is there a problem with his posture?

k   Is the quality of his vision appropriate for the job?

l   Is the quality of his hearing appropriate for the job?

▶ **2   Think and discuss**

With the same partner, make recommendations about the teacher and his environment so that he can reduce accidents and injury and improve productivity.

▶ 3 Read and choose

Read the case study. With a partner, decide which of the recommendations should be put into effect to improve the situation for Joey.

Case study 1

Joey works on a production line. In his job, he uses an electric drill to make small holes in a part of the product. The line makes about 1,500 units of the product each day and it takes five or six seconds for Joey to drill his holes for each unit. Joey is not only using a vibrating tool, he also has poor posture, as when he is drilling, he is stretching out his arm. After a short time, Joey discovered that he had pain in his neck and shoulder. He talked to the health and safety manager, who made some recommendations.

a Replace the drill with a smoother running drill with less vibration.

b Install TV so workers are not bored.

c Increase speed of line to improve productivity.

d Rotate workers on shift to different tasks to reduce exposure to vibration.

e Give workers extra holiday to recover from pain.

f Suspend the drill to support its weight – reducing the vibration.

g Change the production line layout to increase access and improve posture.

h Hold meeting to tell employees to improve posture.

▶ 4 Read and discuss

Work in small groups. Read the case studies below. Make a list of ergonomic recommendations for each case study and then present them to the class.

Case study 2

Freddy is an office worker who frequently uses the telephone and takes messages. He uses a computer for e-mailing and report writing. The computer has a display screen and so is called Display Screen Equipment (DSE). After a few months, Freddy started to have a sore neck and shoulders when he finished work each day. He also frequently had a headache and sore eyes.

Case study 3

Dwayne works in the warehouse as a picker/packer, preparing pallets to leave with orders collected and checked. The environment is very noisy at times but he cannot wear earplugs because he needs to listen for forklifts. He thinks he is going a little deaf and sometimes has ringing in his ears. Also, his knees hurt, as he has to kneel on the floor to reach some items on the bottom shelves of the racking.

Case study 4

Henry works in a workshop with a lot of noisy machinery around. He works a lathe to produce small items needed around ZemTeQ. The work is very repetitive and gives him backache. His eyes are sore and itchy from the sparks. He stands to do his job and has sore feet at the end of the day, meaning that he walks slowly and his productivity falls.

▶ 5 Talk about your own job

a Work in small groups. Ask and answer the questions from Task 1 about your jobs. Make recommendations that might deal with any problems that are mentioned.

b Work with a partner. Discuss the ergonomics of your job and your immediate environment. Can you make any recommendations about your partner's situation?

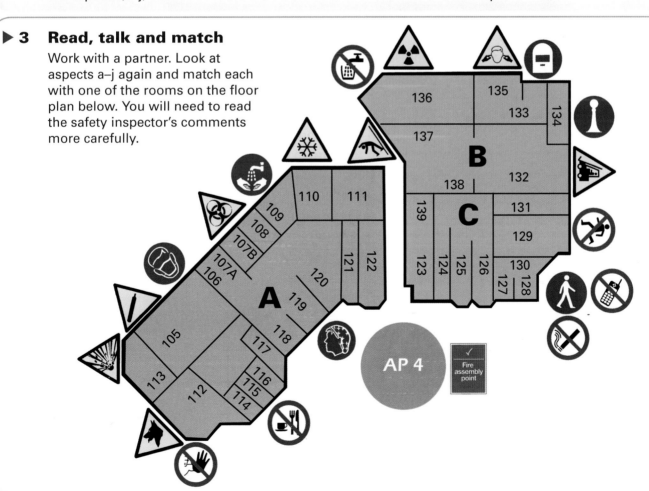

6 | A safety inspector's company tour

Objective: To think about health and safety issues in a working environment.

▶ 1 Look and think

Work with a partner. Look at the aspects of a working environment below. For each aspect, think of a potential health and safety issue.

a display screen equipment (DSE) _2, 18, 21_ _120_

b lighting _____ ____

c ergonomics _____ ____

d noise _____ ____

e vibration _____ ____

f radiation _____ ____

g high temperature _____ ____

h low temperature _____ ____

i welfare and washing facilities _____ ____

j biological hazards _____ ____

Example: *Lighting – the offices are too dark to work in comfortably.*

▶ 2 Read and match

A safety inspector is touring ZemTeQ. Jimmy makes a note of the recommendations that he makes. Read the recommendations (1–30) on page 151 and match them with the aspects (a–j) in Task 1. There are three recommendations for each aspect.

▶ 3 Read, talk and match

Work with a partner. Look at aspects a–j again and match each with one of the rooms on the floor plan below. You will need to read the safety inspector's comments more carefully.

7 Small talk: Repeating and checking

Objective: To learn informal expressions for checking information.

▶ 1 ⊕ 2:24 Listen and write

Listen to the conversation and write the missing words and phrases below.

J Hi. Where are you **1** _____?

R **2** _____? Oh, hello, Jimmy. Sorry, I've got an ear infection so I'm completely deaf today. Can you **3** _____, please?

J I said ... Where are you going?

R Growing? Sorry, can you **4** _____ a little please?

J **5** _____. Do you fancy **6** _____? I'm going to the canteen.

R Supper? A bit early, but I could do with **7** _____. Thanks.

J Excuse me, Richard. Hello? Oh, hi, Paul. Yes, yes, OK, you want to meet for lunch, where? OK, **8** _____ that? O-C-E-A-N-I-A restaurant, yes, yeah, I'll find it. At 12? OK. See you later.

R Was that the boss?

J No, my buddy. He wants to take me to a new restaurant for lunch. Want to come?

R Punch? Sorry, can you **9** _____?

J Lunch, Richard, lunch. **10** _____.

▶ 2 Find and choose

Write 1–10 next to the words and phrases that have a similar meaning to those from the conversation. Use some numbers more than once.

a	going	____	**k**	say that again	____
b	something to eat	____	**l**	on me	____
c	it's not important	____	**m**	speak more loudly	____
d	heading	____	**n**	my turn to pay	____
e	how do you write	____	**o**	not to worry	____
f	sorry	____	**p**	a snack	____
g	slow down a bit	____	**q**	come again	____
h	raise your voice	____			
i	I'm paying	____			
j	a cup of tea	____			

▶ 3 Read and speak

With a partner, act out the conversation several times using different words and phrases from Task 2.

▶ 4 Read and write

a Read the scenarios opposite and choose one.
b With a partner, write out the conversation using words and phrases from Tasks 1 and 2.
c Practise your conversation and then perform it for the class.

You are calling an airline's information line to ask about the price of flights, the types of flights, the departure and arrival times for various destinations. Check your information and check spellings of important words.

You are in a very noisy workshop with your manager. He is giving you instructions for the day. You need to check with him all the information he is giving you, including jobs, places and times.

You call a takeaway restaurant to order some food. You have a very bad telephone line and it's difficult to hear the information being given. Discuss menu options, prices and delivery address.

You are giving directions to a tourist looking for a good local hotel. However, the noise of the traffic means you must both check the information is understood correctly.

The teacher is explaining some grammar to a student in a very noisy classroom with roadworks outside. He must check that the student has understood correctly.

Activate your vocabulary
Go to page 152.

Additional materials

A

Unit 1, Lesson 3, Task 2

Clue	Full question	Answer
last name	*What is your last name?*	
first name		
employee #		
current address		
phone		
how long at address		
emergency contact		
D.O.B.		
certifications		
personal information		

Unit 1, Lesson 6, Task 2

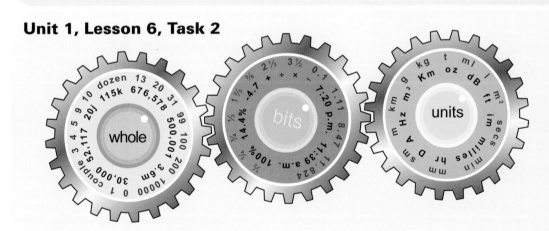

Unit 2, Lesson 1, Task 4

1	risk	hazard	threat	danger
2	dust	fume	gas	oil
3	assessment	precaution	prevention	control
4	thing	stuff	item	object
5	eliminate	reduce	rise	decrease
6	teaching	training	studying	learning
7	accident	incident	mishap	crash
8	tools	ladder	PPE	cable
9	shift	duty	job	task
10	next	after	then	before
11	harmed	injured	hurt	bruise

Unit 2, Lesson 2, Task 2

H&S Risk Assessment	ZemTeQ # 427/b	Date:

Job/Task:

Worker name		Dept./section
Worker #		Tel.
Position		E-mail

Main Hazards
* tick the correct boxes for the job

A EQUIPMENT
entanglement ☐
friction/abrasion ☐
cutting ☐
shearing ☐
stabbing/puncturing ☐
impact ☐
pressure ☐
ejection of part ☐
display equipment ☐
hand tools ☐
B TRANSPORT
work vehicles
mechanical handling ☐
pedestrians ☐
C ACCESS
slips/trips/falls ☐
falling/moving objects ☐
obstruction ☐
work at height ☐
confined space ☐
excavation ☐
D HANDLING
manual handling ☐
mechanical handling ☐

E ELECTRICITY
fixed installation ☐
portable tools/equipment ☐
F CHEMICALS
dust/fume/gas ☐
toxic ☐
irritant ☐
corrosive ☐
carcinogenic ☐
G FIRE/EXPLOSION
flammable material ☐
explosion ☐
means of escape ☐
H PARTICLES & DUST
inhalation ☐
ingestion ☐
skin/eye abrasion ☐
I RADIATION
ionising ☐
non-ionising ☐
J BIOLOGICAL
bacterial ☐
viral ☐
fungal ☐

K ENVIRONMENTAL
noise ☐
vibration ☐
light ☐
humidity ☐
ventilation ☐
temperature ☐
overcrowding ☐
L WORKER
unsuitable for job ☐
long hours ☐
high work rate ☐
violence ☐
unsafe behaviour ☐
stress ☐
young ☐
M OTHER
poor maintenance ☐
no training/info/supervision ☐

Risk Detail
*write some specific detail about the hazards and risk

Persons at Risk
the people **who are at risk and **how** they are at risk*

Consequences
*give possible injuries as a result of the hazards

SIGNATURE:

Unit 2, Lesson 2, Task 3

First	Second	Third	Fourth
TEMPerature	enTANglement	inhaLATion	environMENtal

Unit 2, Lesson 3, Task 4

		Yes	No
1	Is the temperature high in your section?		
2	Do you handle heavy objects?		
3	Do you use more than five hand tools?		
4	Have you slipped or tripped in your section?		
5	Have you had an electric shock at work?		
6	Do you work long hours?		
7	Is your area noisy?		
8	Do you work at height?		
9	Have you heard an explosion at work?		
10	Are vehicles dangerous on your site?		

Unit 2, Lesson 5, Task 3

go up		went up		fall
	fell		will fall	
rise		will jump		dropped
	will level out		will drop	
jump		will stay the same		go down

	Past	Present	Future
⤢			
⬂			
⇨			

Unit 2, Lesson 6, Task 4

Section Meeting   Date:

Agenda

a Choose a restaurant for a section dinner in this town/city.

b What to do to stop lateness in our section.

c How to make people do risk assessments for their jobs.

d What training the section needs.

Unit 2, Lesson 5, Task 3

	continue as before		rose	
continued as before		jumped		will rise
	level out		will go down	
went down		will go up		stay the same
	drop		stayed the same	

	Past	Present	Future
⬀			
⬂			
⇨			

Unit 3, Lesson 1, Task 4

Body part	Hazards	PPE
head		
	loud noise …	
		visors …
lungs		
	chemicals …	
		boots …
skin		
	weather	

Unit 3, Lesson 2, Task 3

PPE instruction sheet

sign

sharp glass

earplugs

gloves

hut

cap

full-face respirator

cable

puddle

dust

safety trainers

steel-capped boots

hairnet

helmet

oil spill

entanglement

disposable dust mask

sunscreen

scaffold

goggles

all weather clothing

ear defenders

strap

resistant gloves

welding

Unit 4, Lesson 2, Task 2

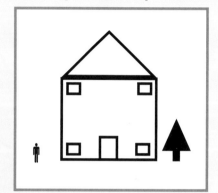

Unit 5, Lesson 2, Task 3

Unit 5, Lesson 3, Task 3

Unit 4, Lesson 2, Task 2

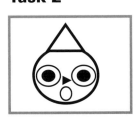

Unit 5, Lesson 5, Task 4

Increase ⬀	Decrease ⬂	Stay between ⬅ ➡

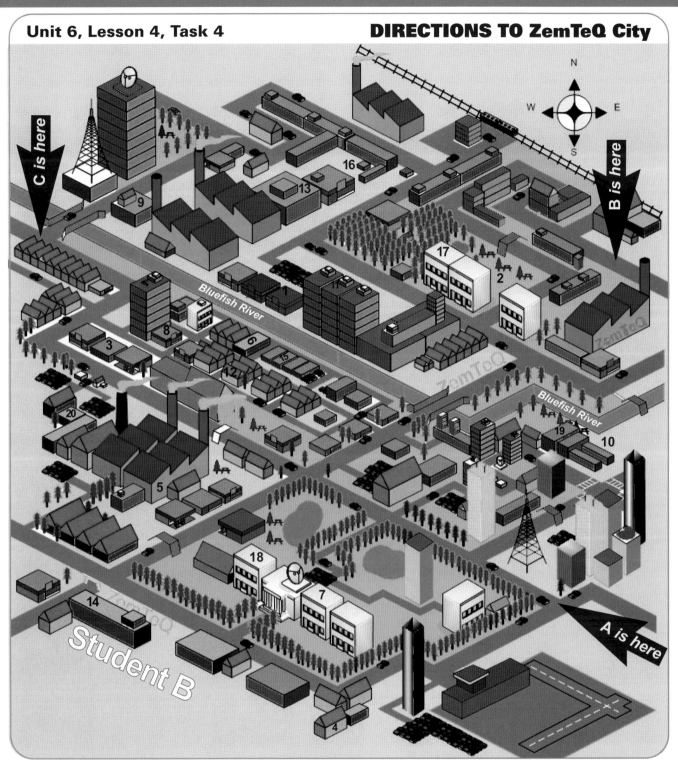

1 Executive Restaurant	**11** Training Centre	**21** Waste Compactor
2 Lunch Area 7	**12** Warehouse 91/b	**22** Maintenance
3 ZemTeQ Bank	**13** Stores	**23** Gas/Petrol Station 3
4 ZemTeQ Travel Agency	**14** Security Head Office	**24** Payroll
5 Plant 3	**15** Canteen 6	**25** R&D
6 Workshop 19	**16** Shower Block 11	**26** Records Office
7 Reception	**17** Administration	**27** Accounts
8 ZemTeQ Medical Centre	**18** HQ	**28** Sales & Marketing
9 Communications Centre	**19** Labs	**29** Pensions Office
10 Human Resources	**20** Quality Control	**30** H&S Headquarters

DIRECTIONS TO ZemTeQ City

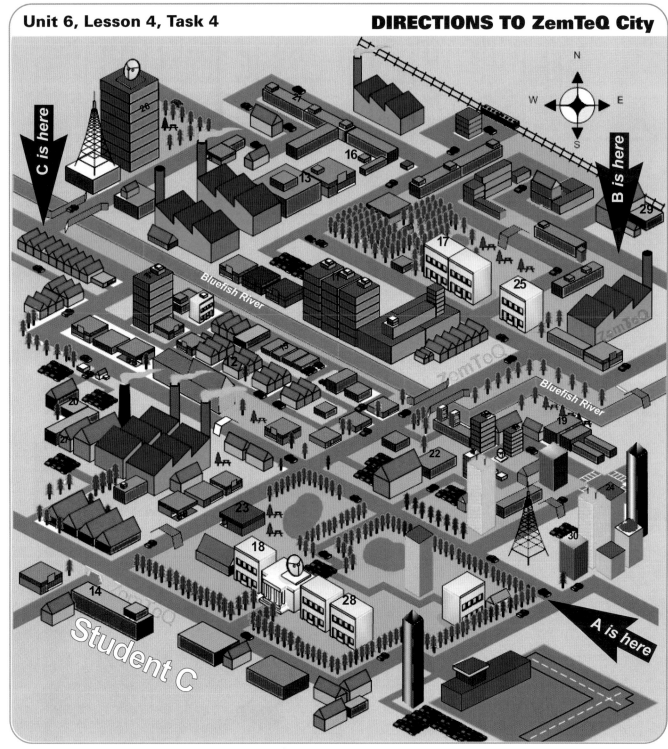

1 Executive Restaurant	**11** Training Centre	**21** Waste Compactor
2 Lunch Area 7	**12** Warehouse 91/b	**22** Maintenance
3 ZemTeQ Bank	**13** Stores	**23** Gas/Petrol Station 3
4 ZemTeQ Travel Agency	**14** Security Head Office	**24** Payroll
5 Plant 3	**15** Canteen 6	**25** R&D
6 Workshop 19	**16** Shower Block 11	**26** Records Office
7 Reception	**17** Administration	**27** Accounts
8 ZemTeQ Medical Centre	**18** HQ	**28** Sales & Marketing
9 Communications Centre	**19** Labs	**29** Pensions Office
10 Human Resources	**20** Quality Control	**30** H&S Headquarters

Unit 6, Lesson 3, Task 5

Starting point (A)	Destination (B)
this room	
	the town centre

Unit 7, Lesson 4, Task 2

Unit 7, Lesson 2, Task 2

A	B	C	D	E
A1 planking	B1 reel	C1 cradle	D1 toe board	E1 adjustable pole
A2 winch	B2 plank	C2 shelf	D2 toe board	E2 rubber footing
A3 lock	B3 rail	C3 leg strap	D3 lock	E3 guard rail
A4 buckle	B4 clamp	C4 crossbar	D4 waist strap	E4 tie-rod
A5 step	B5 truck	C5 tie	D5 rung	E5 chest strap
A6 elbow	B6 foot	C6 arm	D6 platform	E6 guard rail
A7 stile	B7 roller	C7 pole	D7 support foot	E7 guard rail

Unit 7, Lesson 5, Task 4

	Student 1	Student 2	Student 3	Student 4	Student 5
1 How long is your _____?					
2 How hot is _____?					
3 How heavy is _____?					
4 How cold is _____?					
5 How wide is _____?					
6 How tall is _____?					
7 How high is _____?					
8 How old is _____?					
9 How far is _____?					
10 How loud is _____?					
11 How fast _____?					
12 How deep _____?					

Unit 8, Lesson 4, Task 3

HANDLING Risk Assessment	ZemTeQ # 431/e	Date:

Job/Task:

worker name   Dept./section
worker #   Tel.
position   e-mail

Main hazards
tick the correct boxes for the job

risk level?

		yes/no?	high	med	low
Ⓐ **Task Characteristics**					
1	Loads held away from body trunk?				
2	Twisting?				
3	Stooping?				
4	Reaching up?				
5	Vertical movement?				
6	Long carry distance?				
7	Heavy pushing/pulling?				
8	Uncertain load movement?				
10	Short rest time?				
11	High work rate?				
Ⓑ **Load Characteristics**					
1	Heavy?				
2	Bulky?				
3	Difficult to hold?				
4	Unstable?				
5	Harmful (sharp/hot)?				

risk level?

		yes/no?	high	med	low
Ⓒ **Work Environment**					
1	Body position limitations?				
2	Unsuitable floor?				
3	Uneven surface?				
4	Temperature/humidity high?				
5	Insufficient lighting?				
Ⓓ **Worker**					
1	Unusual ability needed?				
2	Health problems?				
3	Training required?				
Ⓔ **Other Factors**					
1	PPE hinders movement?				
2	Incorrect PPE in place?				
3	No planning?				
4	No training/information?				

Persons at risk
*list the people **who** are at risk and **how** they are at risk*

Consequences
give possible injuries as a result of the hazards

SIGNATURE:

Unit 8, Lesson 5, Task 3

Team A

You are ZemTeQ supply managers that buy stock for the company. You need to save money by getting the best price available. Decide on the price you want to pay and the top price you are willing to pay. Negotiate who pays for delivery, who demonstrates the products to the workers and how long the guarantee is for. You are going to negotiate with the other company and give your results to the class.

Item	A	B	C	D	E	F	G
LPG cylinder	100	150	?	?	?	?	?
wooden pallets	220	20	?	?	?	?	?
sack of road salt	10	85	?	?	?	?	?
packet of dust masks	600	10	?	?	?	?	?
box of hand wipes	4000	2	?	?	?	?	?
can of engine lubricant	300	8	?	?	?	?	?
tube of super adhesive	100	6	?	?	?	?	?
can of lemon drink	10,000	1	?	?	?	?	?

Key to grid

A Quantity: number of items you want
B Price: price in the catalogue
C Price: the price you want to pay
D Top price: the most you will pay
E Delivery: who will pay
F Guarantee: how long you want
G Demo: who demonstrates it to workers

Unit 8, Lesson 6, Task 1

Unit 8, Lesson 5, Task 3

Team B

You are the owners of a company supplying items to ZemTeQ. Decide on a name for your company. You need to make money by getting the best price available. Decide on the price you want to sell at and the bottom price you will sell at. Negotiate who pays for delivery and repair. Also, who demonstrates the products to the workers and how long the guarantee is for. Some equipment may need safety instructions, decide who is going to pay for it. You are going to negotiate with the other company and give your results to the class. The best deal in the class wins Business Deal of the Year.

Item	A	B	C	D	E	F	G
LPG cylinder	100	150	?	?	?	?	?
wooden pallets	220	20	?	?	?	?	?
sack of road salt	10	85	?	?	?	?	?
packet of dust masks	600	10	?	?	?	?	?
box of hand wipes	4000	2	?	?	?	?	?
engine lubricant can	300	8	?	?	?	?	?
tube of super adhesive	100	6	?	?	?	?	?
can of lemon drink	10,000	1	?	?	?	?	?

Key to grid

A Quantity: number of items you want
B Price: price in the catalogue
C Price: the price you want to pay
D Top price: the most you will pay
E Delivery: who will pay
F Guarantee: how long you want
G Demo: who demonstrates it to workers

Unit 9, Lesson 2, Task 1

a b c DANGER FLAMMABLE

d e FIRE DOOR

f EMERGENCY Dial 999 FIRE-POLICE AMBULANCE g Fire blanket

h Fire Point

i The Fire Marshal is:

j  EXIT

Unit 9, Lesson 1, Task 2

```
H E A T I N G A P P L I A N C E S O M W
S M O K E R S M A T E R I A L S B V S C
X F F T F L T N E V K U F Q Y O Z A W E
E L E C T R I C A L A P P L I A N C E S
V J B W A H E C G P A L A F B P E J L V
M W I L X U O X M A T C H E S W P L D P
O R C A I A Z D L C P U G O C L B B I K
E L E C T R I C A L S Y S T E M S H N R
V O S S E K K W A T E R H E A T I N G S
M H C O O K I N G E Q U I P M E N T P D
```

Unit 9, Lesson 5, Tasks 2 and 3

On the _____ you need to check the fire escapes; meet with me on the last _____ of the month to talk about it. On Wednesdays you must do a _____, but not on the 15th because you should inspect the _____. On the _____, talk to the fire officers and on the _____, to the fine officers about car parking. On the second Friday and the 27th, check with the shift supervisor about the new _____. The day _____ the hose check, see me about fire procedure posters. There is also a _____ the day before the last fire drill. Take the first _____ off and the last two Saturdays. The second and third Mondays, check the _____ are OK. The day after the _____ truck check, ask Richard to do the fire safety training. You're _____ the other days for football training.

Mon	Tue	Wed	Thur	Fri	Sat	Sun
		1	2	3	4	5
6	7	8	9	10	11	12
13	14	15	16	17	18	19
20	21	22	23	24	25	26
27	28	29	30	31		

Unit 10, Lesson 6, Task 1

Andy   Substance V makes you yawn and feel dizzy.

Randy   Substance W must be kept wet.

Sandy   If Substance X is breathed in, take casualty outside.

Pete   Exposing workers to Substance W multiple times can cause respiratory system problems. It must be stored in an air-conditioned area.

Dean   Substance Y can cause eye problems and can give off poison gas with water.

Owen   Substance X can poison all plants, trees and animals.

John   Substance V must be taken to Waste Stack 19 for disposal.

Jean-Paul   Do not smoke near Substance Y.

Ian   Substance W should not be touched by naked skin, as this can be harmful.

Jack   Substance V might explode if knocked or burnt, and fumes may cause breathing problems. Workers should wear face protection.

Johnny   Do not touch Substance W without gloves.

Wally   Do not pour Substance V down the drain.

Jacques   Substance X burns extremely easily.

Jeremy   Substance Y must be stored below 52°C and there definitely can't be any smoking around it.

Unit 11, Lesson 6, Task 1

Steve	The warehouse electrical fire definitely involved incompetency. Poor old Harry.
Sebastian	Loose connections in one of the machines resulted in it getting too hot.
Sammy	Henry suffered arc burn in the plant area.
Sidney	Not again! Shoddy work led to loose contacts and another low-voltage shock.
Stephen	It's not the first time minor burns have resulted in the warehouse.
Seb	What with workers working without permits and loose connections, no wonder Henny got it!
Samuel	The earth leak current was due to a broken RCD, which Henry should have replaced.
Seamus	Hugh suffered yet another low-voltage shock last week.
Stefan	Howie's quite new. He's never worked in the pipeline, plant, workshop or warehouse.
Shane	Split and worn cable sheaths meant the insulation was damaged and a minor burns injury.
Sid	The death happened in the workshop. His name was Henny, I think.
Scott	Wrongly rated fuses were used in the plant.
Simon	Hugh's worked along the pipeline for years, so should have known about circuit-breakers and spotted loose contacts.
Sylvester	Howie suffered major burns by the storage tanks.
Sandy	The poor maintenance was really due to bad record-keeping and no logs having been filled in.
Stanley	The incompetency was down to unqualified workers. They let Harry down badly.
Spencer	The worker not having a permit to work is definitely a work-system failure.
Sam	Put Henry's injuries down to earth leak current and poor fuses.
Seth	Hugh was the victim of failed breakers not cutting off and loose contacts.
Sean	The reason the earthing wasn't good is that nobody had looked at it for a long time.
Stew	The lack of training and split cable sheaths have been a warehouse problem for ages.
Stuart	Poor work systems and the workshop go hand in hand. No wonder the apparatus overheated.
Sven	The plant workforce need training to rate fuses and spot defective RCDs.
Stan	The damaged circuit-breaker failed to cut off in the pipeline again!

Unit 10, Lesson 2, Task 3

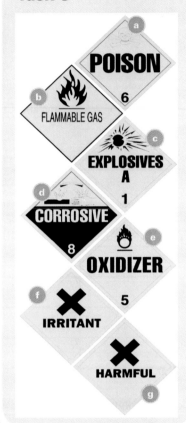

Unit 12, Lesson 5, Task 1

1 tweezers
2 scissors
3 aspirin
4 mask
5 antiseptic
6 Zimmer (frame)
7 scalpel
8 stretcher
9 ophthalmoscope
10 gloves
11 dressing
12 magnifier
13 stethoscope
14 drip
15 drops
16 tape
17 gauze
18 swabs
19 capsule
20 crutches
21 plaster
22 bandages
23 thermometer
24 pill
25 X-ray
26 syrup

Unit 13, Lesson 6, Task 1

Driver 1	The incident with Hans happened at 20 past 4, an hour before Harry's incident.
Supervisor G	Hans hurt his back due to the water on the floor.
Operative 17A	The spill caused the fall on the stairway.
Deputy Supervisor C4	There was only one slip or trip incident in block A last week.
Machine Operator G91	The spinal injury in block A was not very serious.
Shift Manager 3	The lathe incident occurred at 20 past 5 in the afternoon.
Driver's Mate D4	In the report, Harry's cut hand was blamed on a guard not in place.
General Manager	Machine guards will be checked in block E as a result.
CEO	There have been a lot of hand injuries resulting from tools like grinders, drills and lathes recently.
Labourer 92	The incident took place at 5 past 8 and led to a broken arm.
Cleaner Y11	The forklift hit the pedestrian because there was no reversing signal used.
Chief Engineer	Harold was taken from block I to hospital, where they X-rayed his arm.
Quality Inspector 9	No forklifts are used in A, E, O or U.
Picker/packer	Harold finished his shift at 8 p.m., 5 minutes before the accident.
Admin Assistant 82	The incident with Henry happened 5 minutes after the 5 a.m. tea break.
Assistant Manager 4	There were no housekeeping problems in A, E, I, or O.
Electrician 16	The shock resulted in the worker being unconscious with serious burns.
Wages Clerk 9	Housekeeping of electrical equipment has been a problem for the last two months.
Foreman	Henry was out cold for some time due to his incident.
Catering Assistant 12	Tea breaks are at 6 a.m. – except in block U, which is 1 hour earlier.

Unit 14, Lesson 3, Task 3

'A plays golf with all of his bosses and works very hard. He's only had a few accidents.' – SEAN

'Despite working here the longest, B has made few friends. He is usually on time, but is a bit lazy.' – STAN

'I know C has lunch with his supervisor, but he is the grumpiest worker here. However, his work is error-free' – MARK

'A has made a couple of mistakes, but he works at an acceptable rate and is pretty familiar with his post.' – KENT

'B is the most dangerous of the workers, but he has the quickest work rate and knows the most about his job.' - JACK

'C is the slowest worker, but he is the least accident-prone. I think he works harder than B.' – JEFF

'A is always on time. He has been here the shortest time, but is a quick learner. I know he has a technical diploma.' – FRED

'C is the least qualified and his timekeeping is very poor. He is definitely the least informed here.' – GREG

'B is the most qualified, but is the least well known to the management team. He is the least precise or on target with his work.' – CARL

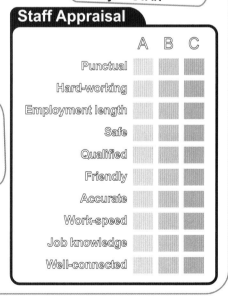

Staff Appraisal

	A	B	C
Punctual			
Hard-working			
Employment length			
Safe			
Qualified			
Friendly			
Accurate			
Work-speed			
Job knowledge			
Well-connected			

Unit 14, Lesson 2, Task 1

1
2
3
4
5
6
7
8
9
10

Unit 14, Lesson 2, Task 2

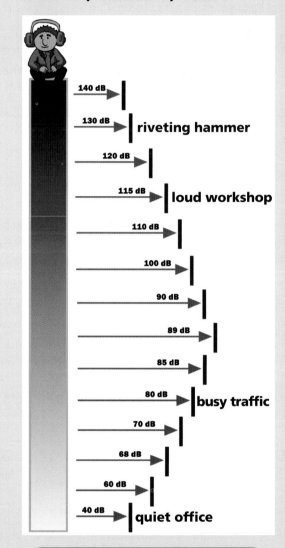

140 dB
130 dB → riveting hammer
120 dB
115 dB → loud workshop
110 dB
100 dB
90 dB
89 dB
85 dB
80 dB → busy traffic
70 dB
68 dB
60 dB
40 dB → quiet office

chainsaw   power drill
normal conversation   loud radio
propeller plane   jet engine
tractor   welding   car engine
heavy site vehicle

Unit 14, Lesson 6, Task 2

1 Long exposure can cause cancer, so I want a sign put there.

2 Please provide foot support and raise the desk height for the office workers in the IT area.

3 I know viruses cause colds, but they also lead to much more serious infections. I want a sign in both A and B parts of the room.

4 I want better seating, or they'll get back pain with the machines shaking so much.

5 Look at the bigger picture. Lighting, temperature, humidity, noise and the whole work process. It's just not working here. I want change. I want it by next week or I close this section, understand?

7 You need some additional external heating in here.

6 The damp and cold in here only make it worse for the workers with drills and chainsaws. I'll bet there's a history of HAVS and VWF.

8 That machine is making a racket. You need to put some damping on it.

10 I want a clear sign because of what is kept here; you know bacteria can cause Legionnaires' disease, TB and tetanus.

16 This area needs to be drier or there'll be problems with fungi and moulds leading to asthma, athlete's foot or farmer's lung.

11 You need to improve work rotation, maintenance and fault reporting to reduce WBV here. I also want a slip hazard sign because of oil on the floor.

9 Need to put drinking water next to no-running area to avoid heatstroke and overheating in this enclosed space.

12 The temperature is too high to keep body temperature at 37°C.

13 It's too low. The workers will lose heat quickly and it may lead to possible frostbite.

15 I want a sign for it and workers wearing a dosemeter. If it gets too high it will be serious!

30 It's too loud mate! You'll have to reduce the volume somehow.

14 Focus on the body, abilities and competence of the worker, and how they 'fit' with the controls and gauges of the equipment.

19 Not only should there be warm water and soap, but also towels or hand driers in a well-lit and ventilated area.

18 You know that computer monitor work can lead to eye strain and headaches, you need better lighting to let workers read the documents.

26 They need to wear extra thick warm clothing and have frequent rest periods so they can use the washrooms next door.

17 You must put washing and sanitary facilities here and put a sign between the cold store and biological hazard.

28 Short exposure can cause vomiting, burns and death. Protection is vital!

27 You must have suitable and sufficient lighting in here as there are forklifts about. It's very hazardous.

29 You need an emergency backup and more lamps to stop slips, trips and falls.

20 You definitely need a sign with all the banging in here and the welding next door.

21 The seating at the computer terminals needs to have adjustable height. You need to improve the office workers' area next to the room that needs hairnet signs, I can't remember the number.

22 You need to improve natural lighting in case of a power cut. So keep the windows and skylights clean.

24 I want a no-access and guard dog sign outside and, more importantly for you, to re-think the whole worker and environment situation here. You have serious ergonomic issues here.

23 Need to put in ventilation so workers can sweat and cool off.

25 The facilities need to include water closets, wash stations and urinals.

Activate your vocabulary

Below is a series of activities that will help you transfer the vocabulary in the unit so that it becomes part of your active vocabulary. You can decide as a class which activities interest you; there's no need to do it all.

Letter focus

1 Write it
Listen to the teacher and write the words he/she says below.

1 _____	26 _____
2 _____	27 _____
3 _____	28 _____
4 _____	29 _____
5 _____	30 _____
6 _____	31 _____
7 _____	32 _____
8 _____	33 _____
9 _____	34 _____
10 _____	35 _____
11 _____	36 _____
12 _____	37 _____
13 _____	38 _____
14 _____	39 _____
15 _____	40 _____
16 _____	41 _____
17 _____	42 _____
18 _____	43 _____
19 _____	44 _____
20 _____	45 _____
21 _____	46 _____
22 _____	47 _____
23 _____	48 _____
24 _____	49 _____
25 _____	50 _____

2 Order it
Put these words in alphabetical order. Quickly!

3 Spell it
Work with a partner. Student A reads the words and Student B spells the words. Quickly!

Sound focus

4 Rhyme it
Group the words that rhyme.

5 Stress it
Mark the words to show their stress: 1st, 2nd or 3rd syllable?

6 Pronounce it
Work with a partner. Student A spells a word and Student B must pronounce it correctly.

7 Mouth it
Work with a partner. Take it in turns to mouth words while the other guesses which word it is.

Meaning focus

8 Class it
In groups: decide which words are nouns (N), verbs (V), adjectives (A) and other (O).

9 Ask it
With a partner, ask questions about the words depending on which class (N, V, A or O) they are. Use the table opposite.

10 Explain it
In groups, one student reads the words, the others say if the word is good or bad. Explain your thinking to your group.

11 Draw it
In groups, each person draws a selection of the words. The other students guess what it represents.

Noun	Verb	Adjective	Other
1 What is a/an _____?	**1** Who or what _____s?	**1** Who is _____?	**1** What ...?
2 Where can I find a/an _____?	**2** What hazards are there with _____ing?	**2** What is the opposite of _____?	**2** Where ...?
3 How do I use a/an _____?	**3** Where do you _____?	**3** What is _____?	**3** When ...?
4 What are the dangers with _____?	**4** Can you mime _____ing?	**4** Are you _____?	**4** Who ...?

Fluency focus

12 Phone it
Work with a partner. Role-play a phone conversation with a co-worker. How many words can you mention in two minutes?

13 Personalize it
Mark words relevant to your job. Using these words, talk to your group for two minutes.

14 Write it
Using the new words, write your job description or SOP for your job tasks, or write an e-mail to a co-worker.

15 Act it
In front of the class, pretend to be your manager telling a trainee about their new job. Use as many new words as you can.

16 Sketch it
Sketch a scene, illustrating as many of the words as possible, then dictate this scene to other students. Compare drawings.

Play focus

17 Bingo it
Put words in the grid and play bingo with the class.

18 Crossword it
With a partner, make a crossword.

19 Wordsearch it
Make a wordsearch.

20 Concentrate
Follow your teacher's instructions to play *concentration* in teams. Then fill in the grid from memory after the game.

	A	B	C	D	E
1					
2					
3					
4					
5					

21 Describe it
Work with a partner. In front of the class, Student A describes a word and Student B must guess it. Each pair has two minutes.

22 Memorize it
Play the memory game. You have two or three minutes to memorize the words. You will then have two minutes in front of the class to say as many as possible.

23 Article it
Write a magazine article. Try to use as many of the words as you can.

24 Hit it
The teacher will put your definitions on the board. He/she will read out the words and your group representative must run and hit the correct definitions.

Word list

L

lacerated	12
ladder	1
leak	8
load	1
location	13
lubricant	8

M

maintain	3
maintenance	6
malfunction	11
mallet	4
mandatory	5
manual	1
mask	3
match	9
mechanical	1
medicine	12

N

naked flame	9
near miss	13
non-slip	7
numbness	14

O

overreach	7
overturn	8
oxygen source	9

P

painkiller	12
pallet	8
pedestrian	1
permit to work	1
planking	7
poison	10
pole	7
pollution	14

posture	14
powder	9
power tool	4
PPE	1
precaution	2
pressure	5
prevent	2
procedure	9
prohibition	5
protect	3
pulse	11
purpose	4

R

radiation	1
rail	6
ramp	8
react	10
recommendation	13
recovery position	11
resistant	3
responsible	3
restrict (v)	13
result	13
resuscitation	11
risk	2
risk assessment	1
RSI	14
rung	7

S

sack truck	8
saw	4
scaffold	2
scales	5
screwdriver	4
secure	7
sharp edge	5
shock	11
site	6
slip	2
slippery	8

solvent	10
sore	12
speed limit	6
speedometer	5
spillage	1
splinter	12
split	7
sprain	8
stabbing	5
stable	7
stairway	6
static	9
stationary	6
steel-capped	3
stepladder	7
stoop	8
store	3
strain	8
strap	7
substance	10
substandard	13
supervisor	5
supply	11
surface	5
switch	4
swollen	12

T

thermometer	5
tighten	3
timer	5
toe board	7
toxic	10
trestle	7
trigger	4
trip	2
twist	8

U

unconscious	12
unplug	4

V

vapour	10
ventilation	10
vibration	4
victim	11
volume	5
vomit	12

W

walkway	6
warehouse	6
warning	3
welding equipment	9
welfare	14
winch	7
witness	13
workshop	1
wrench	4

Transcripts

▶ CD1 Track 1
Unit 1, Lesson 3, Task 1
Listen and write

You are going to listen to health and safety lectures throughout this course. Your lecturer is Richard. Listen to Richard introduce himself and fill in his Employee Information Card (EIC).

Good morning. Welcome to the first ZemTeQ health and safety training session. Let me tell you a little about myself. My name is Richard, Richard Devonshire – you can call me Richard. I am a health and safety training manager. I have been in this job for 15 years, so if you have a question, please put your hand up and ask me. Your first job today is to fill in the Employee Information Card so I know more about you. I will give you my information as an example.

The first section is basic name and address. So, my last name is Devonshire, spelt D-E-V-O-N-S-H-I-R-E, and my first name is Richard, that's R-I-C-H-A-R-D. My employee number is 67420E. You all have a number for your company. My current address is 12, High London Road in London. The zip or post code is NW12 64T. My mobile is 870 555479217, which you should only use in emergencies. There is also my office number: 012705 62462434. The previous address where I lived before London Road was 194 Green Grass Avenue. I have lived at my current address for about five years and three months.

Now, if you have an accident, we must call your friends, family or boss, so, tell us now who you want us to call. For me, call my son Alex Devonshire at 147, Chelsea Fields Lane, London, on 870 555628499, extension 1043.

The third section is just a little personal information. My date of birth is 9th May, 1962, just joking, '52. And, of course, I'm male. Obviously, I have been employed here before, starting on my birthday in 1995. Clearly, I have several special certifications and clearances because of my job, including a Health and Safety Inspection Diploma and an Accident Investigator Licence. The last section is voluntary personal information. So only put what you want. For me, I play tennis at the weekend and swim every day. I am married and am in good health. Thanks guys. Now it's your turn.

▶ Track 2
Unit 1, Lesson 4, Task 1
Listen and write

Listen to Richard give an outline of a health and safety course.

a Write down the 14 main topics he will cover.

OK, guys, thanks for filling in the Employee Information Cards. Good work. Now I will introduce the course to you, which is in 14 separate parts.

To begin, we will look at general workplace health and safety, which is like an introduction to all the other parts, with common terms and ideas from the other units.

Secondly, we will talk about risk assessment, which helps us plan to stop hazards and lower risk in our jobs. You need to think about this for every job you do, from day one.

Thirdly, we will read about Personal Protective Equipment (PPE), which is to protect workers from hazards, and to lower risk. You should know what you need, and why you need it, at all times.

Next, we will discuss equipment safety for hand-held tools and equipment. An important subject, as I know you all use tools in your job. Do you know how to use them correctly? Mmm, we'll see.

After that, we will speak about equipment safety for mechanical equipment, which includes anything from large powered items to conveyor belts. We all use those, even if it is only at the supermarket checkout.

Then, we will think about transport safety for both pedestrians and vehicles. Do you know how to cross the road? Do you know how to reverse around a corner? Then why do so many people have to go to hospital because of these simple things?

For the seventh subject, we go through working at height, you know, ladders and scaffolding mainly. Do you know the procedure for setting up a ladder? We all think we do. So why are there so many accidents?

Following that, we will see an explanation of handling, both manual and mechanical. It's more than muscles, you know; you must use your brain as well.

Coming after that, I will spell out the main points of fire safety in the workplace, including fire extinguishers, the fire triangle and fire procedures. Do you know how many die in workplace fires every year? Well, it's too many.

After, I will explain chemical safety, including hazardous substances commonly met at work. And no, I don't mean the food in the canteen.

Later, I will describe electrical safety, covering electric shock hazards and equipment checks. Can you wire a plug? Do you know what each colour wire is? Many don't, now that's really shocking!

The twelfth session will include information about first aid, taking in common injuries and treatment. Hands up anyone who has had a broken arm or leg recently. One … two … three … Yep, that's quite high. You need to start thinking.

Afterwards, we will detail incidents and accidents, mainly practising report-writing for all you Sherlock Holmes people out there.

Lastly, we will concentrate on other hazards, which covers noise, ergonomics and radiation, for example. We all have noisy neighbours, are you one? Can you reduce the risk?

So, I hope that's clear. Does anybody have any questions?

▶ Track 3
Unit 1, Lesson 7, Task 1
Listen and write

Listen to the conversation between Richard and one of his students and write the missing words and phrases.

J Hello, are you here for the course?

R Yes, I am. I'm the teacher. My name's Richard.

J Oh, nice to meet you, Richard, I'm Jimmy. Do you work in the health and safety department at ZemTeQ, or are you from another company?

R I'm from another training company, but I have worked at ZemTeQ for years. Which department do you work in, Jimmy?

J I'm a new trainee in health and safety. I've been at ZemTeQ for two weeks now. I like the work, but I don't like the early mornings.

R What about the holidays and other benefits? I thought ZemTeQ was pretty good.

J Yeah, it's OK. I get three weeks' vacation a year. So, Richard, can I get your e-mail address to ask any questions about the course?

R Sure, Jimmy, it's devonshire@hnstraining.com. Anyway, I've got to go and get ready. See you later, Jimmy.

▶ Track 4
Unit 2, Lesson 1, Task 2
Listen and write

You are going to listen to Richard giving a lecture which introduces risk assessment. Listen and write the missing words and phrases.

Good morning. I hope you are all well and ready to look at some health and safety. Today, we will talk about risk assessment, which helps us know what to do to stop accidents happening. Risk assessment helps us to think about eliminating hazards and reducing risks. Let me clarify a few terms here. A hazard is something that causes harm, for example, a chemical or using a ladder. A risk is the chance a person is harmed or injured by the hazard.

Generally, we do a risk assessment by going through the following steps:

First, look for the hazards that might cause serious harm or injury to people. For example, slipping or tripping, fire, chemicals, moving machinery, working at height, vehicles, electricity, dust and fumes, handling, noise and poor lighting. That's just to name a few. So you need to be thinking, thinking, thinking.

Next, decide who is at risk and how they are at risk. There are always more people than you think: trainees, cleaners, the boss. Stop and think before you do the job.

After this, evaluate the risk level, usually written as low, medium or high risk. Decide if precautions are adequate or if more should be done, for example, by eliminating the job, substituting the item, changing the work method, reducing exposure time, adding engineering controls, using good housekeeping, using safe systems of work, doing extra training, using PPE, and so on.

The next step is to keep a written record of the risk assessment. Other people will want to look at your decisions. You might want to look at what you wrote a year ago, so you can do the job better now.

Finally, review the risk assessment after some time, or if there is an accident or incident, or even a change in the machine being used to do a job.

▶ **Track 5**
Unit 2, Lesson 5, Task 1
Listen and draw
Listen to the teacher describe Jimmy's levels of happiness during the week. Draw a graph to illustrate Jimmy's week.

Jimmy started the week with a score of six because he felt OK after the weekend and a family meal. His happiness level dropped to a four on Monday, because it was Monday. It jumped to nine on Tuesday, after he was given a surprise promotion, but fell to two the next day, when his boss said it was a mistake. The following day, his mood rose to seven as he spent time with his friends in a restaurant. On Friday, it continued at seven because it was Friday and the end of the working week. Also, he had plans to go fishing at the weekend. His mood decreased to two the next day as he sat fishing all day on the river and caught nothing. His happiness level went up to ten on Sunday because he caught a huge fish then cooked it on his barbecue for his friends, and then had an early night and slept well.

▶ **Track 6**
Unit 2, Lesson 5, Task 2
Listen and write
Listen again to the teacher describing Jimmy's week and write the missing words.
[repeat of Track 5]

▶ **Track 7**
Unit 2, Lesson 7, Task 1
Listen and write
Listen to the conversation and write the missing words and phrases.

R Good morning, Jimmy. How are you doing?
J Oh, hi, Richard. I'm good. And you?
R Not bad. Did you have a good week?
J Yes, I learnt a lot last week, you know, new people, new jobs. You?

R A difficult week. We had some problems. New computers, then the car broke down, but the weekend was good. How was your weekend?
J Busy. We went shopping and had a family meal at my house. I studied a lot for this new job and watched a few movies.
R Did you go to that new shopping mall out of town?
J Yes, it's huge. I went to about 30 or 40 shops. I was so tired … and broke. Oh, by the way, thanks for answering my e-mail questions.
R No problem. Anytime. Are you enjoying the course?
J Definitely. So what are we doing this week?
R Aha, surprise. I'll tell you later.

▶ **Track 8**
Unit 3, Lesson 1, Task 3
Listen and answer
Listen to the lecture and mark if the sentences are true (T) or false (F).

Hello, everybody. Good to see you again. I hope you've had lots of coffee and are not too sleepy. Let's begin. Today I will talk about PPE, that is Personal Protective Equipment, which is worn to prevent injury or harm to workers' bodies.

PPE must be suitable for the hazard, made of material resistant to the hazard, suitable for the person, and strong. Let's look at the main types of PPE available to workers. Firstly, the head faces many hazards like falling objects, working in small spaces and hair entanglement. Hard hats, helmets, bump caps or hairnets can be used as PPE. Loud or long noises can be a hazard for hearing, so we use earplugs, ear defenders or earmuffs.

Our eyes are so important. There are many hazards such as dust, flying particles or welding. We can use safety glasses, goggles or visors and shields in some situations.

We also need to protect our lungs, which we use to breathe. Sometimes we find hazards like dirt, fumes, gas, vapours or situations with little oxygen. We must use dust masks, face masks, respirators or breathing apparatus PPE to control the hazards.

Without our hands, it would be difficult to work, so we must protect them. Sharp objects, chemicals and extreme temperatures are all hazards to think about. So, we need to choose gloves that are protective, resistant or insulating.

There are many hazards to our feet too, for example: slipping, sharp objects, falling objects and chemicals. We use PPE like steel-toecap safety shoes, safety clogs, safety trainers or boots to protect our feet and toes.

Skin protection is to be thought about at all times – using sunscreen or suncream, barrier cream and impermeable barriers, like aprons. We need to protect against dirt and corrosives as well as sun exposure and solvents. The whole body and trunk need overalls, boiler suits and specialized clothing like high-visibility suits and heat-resistant clothing. These protect against so many hazards in your workplace like chemicals, vehicles, extreme temperatures and weather.

So, everybody, I ask you to think. Yes, think very long and hard about the hazards you face, and choose your PPE carefully. It could save your life and that of your co-workers.

▶ **Track 9**
Unit 3, Lesson 1, Task 4
Listen and write
Listen to the lecture again and complete the table with all the main body areas which require PPE, the hazards they face and the type of PPE used to protect them.
[repeat of Track 8]

▶ **Track 10**
Unit 3, Lesson 7, Task 1
Listen and write
Listen to the conversation and write the missing words and phrases.

J Hello, Richard. Oh, it's so hot today, isn't it?

R I prefer it cooler, don't you? How was your week?

J Pretty good. I tried to find that new fish restaurant on Saturday. Do you know where it is?

R Erm … yes. It's near that new pool on the other side of town. So, turn left after the lights by the pool. Carry on for a mile or so, take the next right and it's between the bank and the coffee shop.

J So, that's left, one mile, right, and next to the bank, right?

R Yep, that's right. It's a great restaurant. I recommend the shellfish.

J Thanks, Richard. I'm getting a coffee, do you want one? On me.

R Thank you, Jimmy. Milk and four sugars. Wow, it's very, very hot today!

J What will the weather be like this weekend?

R I don't know. I guess it will be hot again. Anyway, let's get that coffee.

▶ **Track 11**
Unit 4, Lesson 1, Task 3
Listen and answer
a Listen to the lecture and answer the questions.

Good morning. Today's subject is hand-held tools, which need to be correct for the job, well maintained and properly used. I'll break this subject into two parts.

Firstly, non-powered hand-held tools. Many accidents are caused by misuse or poor maintenance, including: broken handles, incorrect use of cutting tools, poor-quality handles, splayed spanners, chipped or loose hammer heads and poorly insulated tools. These common problems lead to many injuries.

Three controls are used to prevent injury:

a Suitability – tools are suitable for purpose.

b Inspection – regular checks, discarding or repair of tools, correct storage and locking away when not in use.

c Training – is required for all tool use, before using them.

Secondly, hand-held power tools. We will cover electrical hazards another time. Some of the main hazards include: mechanical entanglement; flying waste material; contact with cutting blades; hitting gas, electrical or water services; manual handling problems with heavy tools; hand/arm vibration; tripping hazards from cables; explosion risk with petrol-driven tools; and high noise levels and dust.

▶ **Track 12**
Unit 4, Lesson 1, Task 3
Listen and answer
b Complete the phrases from the lecture.
Listen again and check your answers.
[repeat of Track 11]

► **Track 13**

Unit 4, Lesson 1, Task 4

Listen and choose

What did Richard say: a or b?

[repeat of Track 11]

► **Track 14**

Unit 4, Lesson 7, Task 1

Listen and write

Listen to the conversation and write the missing words and phrases.

J Hello, Richard. Good week?

R Yep, and you? How is it going in ZemTeQ's health and safety department?

J OK, a lot of hard work. I'm going to the capital on a report-writing course next week, then I'm going to attend some meetings at HQ the week after.

R Busy is better than bored, Jimmy. Are you going to attend my course next week?

J Not sure. I'll send you an e-mail this week. Sorry about that.

R Don't worry. The week after next I'm going on holiday, so you won't be marked absent then.

J Oh, where are you going on holiday? Somewhere hot?

R No, I'm not. I don't like the hot weather so much. I'm going to go skiing in the mountains up north. Are you going to go on holiday this year, Jimmy?

J I'm going to visit my uncle on the coast and go fishing every day. I love it.

R That sounds great. Shall we go into the class?

J Sure. After you, Richard. Last week's class was great. I liked …

► **Track 15**

Unit 5, Lesson 1, Task 2

Listen and answer

Listen to Richard's lecture on mechanical equipment safety and answer the questions.

Hello, is everybody ready? Can you … er … yes you, be quiet at the back? OK, let's begin. Today is machine safety. Moving machinery can cause injury in many ways; we will look at them later. First, let's think of ways to prevent machine accidents: the control measures.

Firstly, guards. These must be used to prevent access to dangerous parts. They can be plastic or wire mesh, for example. If fixed guards are not possible, then other methods are used like trip systems, photosensitive devices and pressure-sensitive materials. When guards cannot give full protection, use jigs, holders or push sticks.

Secondly, machine operation is an important subject. If the workers are young or inexperienced, they might need more supervision. Trained operators must think about PPE, which can be different for each machine. And remember, the machine must be well lit to see properly and safely.

Next, machinery maintenance, which makes sure guards and devices are checked and in working order. If you remove a guard during maintenance, make sure you stop the machine with a device like a lock-off system so that it cannot be restarted. And think … never, ever try and get round the guards when you operate them.

On to machine controls. Make sure they are clearly labelled: stop, start, etc. Also, you must know where the emergency stop controls are. Very importantly, never cover the controls – they could get pushed accidentally.

Finally, the operator's checklist. Yes, that means you! Five dos to think about:

1 know where the stop button is

2 put guards in position when you use the machine

3 keep the area around the machine clean and tidy

4 report faults

5 wear your PPE

And five don'ts:

1 don't use it if you are not authorized

2 never clean a moving machine

3 never use it if it has a danger sign on it

4 never wear chains, loose clothing, rings or have long hair; and

5 never, ever, ever talk to people when using a machine

► **Track 16**

Unit 5, Lesson 1, Task 3

Listen and circle

Look at the pairs of words in the circles and listen to the four control measures again.

[repeat of Track 15]

▶ **Track 17**

▶ Track 17

Unit 5, Lesson 1, Task 4

Listen and tick

Listen again to Richard's dos and don'ts checklist at the end of his lecture. Which of the following are dos and which are don'ts?

[repeat of Track 15]

▶ Track 18

Unit 5, Lesson 7, Task 1

Listen and write

Listen to the conversation between Jimmy and a shop assistant and write the missing words and phrases.

SA Good morning. Can I help you?

J Yes, I have a complaint. There is a problem with the TV I bought here last week. It's not working.

SA What exactly is the matter with it?

J Well, firstly, it doesn't turn on sometimes. And secondly, the plug gets very hot.

SA So ... what exactly do you want us to do with it, sir?

J Well, you can repair it, give me my money back, or give me a new one.

SA I can replace it for you immediately, sir.

J Thank you, but can you hurry up, please? I have an appointment to go to.

SA Certainly, if you can wait just a minute, sir.

▶ Track 19

Unit 6, Lesson 1, Task 2

Listen and answer

Listen to Richard's lecture on transport safety for pedestrians. What four types of hazard does he mention?

Hello, I hope you are all well today. This morning, we will look at transport safety, especially the safety of pedestrians – that is, people walking about. We looked at hazards in the last unit, so now we will think about how to prevent accidents.

First of all, avoiding slips, trips and falls. Risk assessments are important and you – the workers – should be thinking about uneven floors, badly lit stairways, puddles from leaking roofs and staying in the correct walkways. You must record all cleaning and maintenance work and make sure anti-slip covers are on stairs, ladders and walkways. And remember ... use warning signs for washed floors.

Secondly, falls from height. Guard rails and barriers will prevent many falls, also fencing, toe boards and, sometimes, safety nets. Banisters or handrails on stairways should always be used, and holes in floors filled or fenced. Key to preventing accidents is: using non-slip surfaces, good lighting and maintenance.

Thirdly, collisions with moving vehicles injure many people in and out of work every year. It is important to separate pedestrians and vehicles and have clear walkways and clearly marked pedestrian crossings. Entrances, exits and blind corners to buildings are accident black spots, so the use of guard rails and barriers by workers is very important. Loading and unloading areas are also black spots and speed limits must be used.

Finally, preventing accidents caused by striking against fixed or stationary objects. Simple. Use good lighting – yes, just turn it on. Use the walkways. Know what signs mean and – how many times have I said it? – use your PPE.

▶ Track 20

Unit 6, Lesson 1, Task 3

Listen and write

Listen to the lecture again and try to complete as many gaps in the transcript as you can.

[repeat of Track 19]

▶ Track 21

Unit 6, Lesson 7, Task 1

Listen and write

Listen to the conversation and write the missing words and phrases.

J Good morning, Richard. Have you heard the news?

R Good morning. No, what's happened?

J Well, the new furnace in Plant 3 has blown up.

R When did it happen?

J It blew up about ten last night.

R Was anyone injured?

J Yeah. Three guys went to hospital with serious burns.

R What caused the incident?

J Well, it's only gossip, but people say the engineer fell asleep on shift. He's such a lazy man.

R Jimmy, you shouldn't believe gossip. Let's wait for the incident report. However, have you heard about the new manager in stores? He …

► **Track 22**

Unit 7, Lesson 3, Task 1

Listen and answer

Listen to the first part of Richard's lecture on ladder safety and note down your answers to the three questions.

Hello, everyone, hope you are having a good day. Let's get down to business. Today, we will talk about hazards with working at height, and more specifically, access equipment. Let's focus on ladders to start with.

The number one cause of accidents with ladders is ladder movement, when they are not secured to a fixed point, especially at the foot. Other causes include overreaching, slipping on a rung and ladder defects.

Normally, two types of materials are used to make ladders:

1 Aluminium ladders are light, so be careful in strong winds.

2 Timber (wooden) ladders need regular inspection for damage and should not be painted, which can hide cracks.

► **Track 23**

Unit 7, Lesson 3, Task 2

Listen and write

Listen to the second part of the lecture and complete the ZemTeQ ladder safety advice.

Remember, when you use a ladder:

1 Ask yourself or your supervisor: Is the ladder the best access to the job?

2 Check the location. The supporting wall and ground should be dry.

3 Make sure it is stable. The inclination should be 1–4, or about 75 degrees.

4 Tie the foot to a strong support.

5 Check weather conditions. Wind and heavy rain are dangerous.

6 Have at least 1 metre of ladder above the step-off point.

7 Avoid overreaching.

8 Place paints and tools in a secure place.

9 Climb by using both hands.

10 Wear non-slip footwear.

11 Clean and dry all dirty rungs.

12 Inspect ladder for damage.

13 Maintain ladder regularly.

14 Transport carefully, ladders damage easily.

15 Store it in a dry place.

► **Track 24**

Unit 7, Lesson 7, Task 1

Listen and write

Listen and write the missing words and phrases.

Did you see that programme last night?

Excuse me, don't I know you?

Is this taken?

Haven't seen you for ages.

Nice day, isn't it?

See the game last night, Dave?

Got a light, mate?

Hello, could you give me a hand?

Have you finished reading that?

Can I borrow a few euros?

Have you heard the one about …?

What are you up to?

Got anything on this weekend?

Fancy popping round later?

Guess what?

► **CD2 Track 1**

Unit 8, Lesson 1, Task 3

Listen and correct

Listen to Richard's lecture about manual handling.

a Mark the statements from Task 2 as correct (✓) or incorrect (✗).

Welcome. It's good to see you again. Today's session is about manual handling, which is responsible for a large number of workplace injuries … and makes me so angry!

Did you know that a quarter of all accidents come from manual handling, and that these usually involve more than three days off work? Normally, these include sprains, strains, cuts, fractures and amputations. Many of these result from spending a long time lifting, rather than a specific accident.

People should ask: 'Do I really need to lift this at all?'… not, 'How do I lift this safely?' But workers don't listen, and 80% will have a back injury at some time. Did you know that cold weather and old age mean injury is more probable? I tell people every day, stooping or bending forward during a lift means a hernia is more likely. I tell them to take a break, turn on lights and use better housekeeping. Ignoring these three points often results in the objects being carried falling to the ground.

Remember, handling includes lifting, pushing, pulling and carrying, and that body stress is higher for pushing than pulling. I repeat to people, carrying weight in front is more spinal stress than if it is carried on the back. They don't listen. I say again and again, gripping and loading close to the body is important. So many unnecessary injuries. Don't very fat people know back injuries happen more to them than thin people? Twisting, stooping and reaching are all wrong, very wrong. Take a rest; you need to rest once in a while. Listen carefully: avoid heavy, bulky, unstable, sharp or hot loads – it's dangerous. Are you listening?!

Think about the floor; watch out for uneven, slippery or wet floors and strong gusts. You must get a good grip, think about foot position, bend your knees, not your back, and keep your chin tucked in. And finally, remember, you are different from your friend. Your age, strength, fitness and size are all important in manual handling. OK, I've finished. Did you listen? Probably not!

▶ **Track 2**
Unit 8, Lesson 1, Task 4
Solve the puzzle
Look at the clues and complete the crossword using key words from the lecture. Then listen to the lecture again to check your answers.
[repeat of Track 1]

▶ **Track 3**
Unit 8, Lesson 7, Task 1
Listen and write
Listen to the conversation and write the missing words and phrases.

J Hello, Richard. Need a hand?

R Morning, Jimmy. Could you get the door for me, please?

J No problem. You've got a lot of books. Let me help.

R Thanks. Why don't we go to the canteen for a coffee? We are very early for class.

J Good idea. I need something to wake up.

R I had an idea yesterday. Why don't we organize a class trip to a restaurant? Any suggestions?

J We could go to that fish place by the market in the centre of town. I heard the food is excellent and quite reasonable.

R The problem is that a lot of people don't like fish. Would you ask people today what they prefer?

J OK. Why don't I drop you a line later in the week to let you know?

R That would be great. Now, why don't you tell me what we did in the last session?

J OK. We talked about …

▶ **Track 4**
Unit 9, Lesson 3, Task 1
Listen and write
Listen to the first part of Richard's lecture on fire safety and note down your answers to the three questions.

Good morning, everybody. I hope everyone's awake and ready to start. Today's subject is fire safety. There are six general types of fire:

The first is Class A. This involves solid materials like wood, paper, furniture and plastics. These fires are extinguished by cooling with water.

The second type is Class B. This includes liquids such as paints, oil or fats.

Type B1 are fires with liquids soluble in water, like methanol, and are put out by CO_2, dry powder and water spray.

Type B2 are fires with liquids not soluble in water, like petrol and oil. We use foam and B1 extinguishers to put these out.

Class C fires involve gases like butane or propane. They are extinguished by using foam or dry powder with water to cool nearby containers.

Class D involves metals like magnesium or aluminium. Special dry powder extinguishers are used on these.

Class F – yes, F, not E – is next. These are fires with high-temperature cooking oils in food shops, canteens or restaurants.

The last type are electrical fires, involving electrical equipment. CO_2 or dry powder extinguishers are used on these types of fires.

We will talk more about fire extinguishers later, as well as the fire triangle.

▶ **Track 5**
Unit 9, Lesson 3, Task 2
Listen and complete
Listen to the lecture again and complete the table with the missing information.
[repeat of Track 4]

▶ **Track 6**
Unit 9, Lesson 7, Task 1
Listen and write
Listen to the conversation and write the missing words and phrases.

J Hi, Richard. Can I talk to you? I need some advice.

R Oh, hi, Jimmy. Sure. What's the matter?

J I'm not sure what to do. I have been offered two jobs, one in the health and safety office and the other as part of the investigation team on site. Which is better?

R Well, I think both have a lot of upsides. A big plus for the office is that it's safe, clean and comfortable. On the other hand, it can be boring if you're an active person.

J Yeah, I agree. I like walking round the site and chatting to the guys. But it's not so good in bad weather.

R Yes, but generally speaking, the outdoor job will be different every day. It will be more interesting.

J I guess. I need to think it over.

R Good idea. Why not write two lists? Write the advantages and disadvantages and then decide.

J Thanks, Richard. I appreciate your advice.

▶ **Track 7**
Unit 10, Lesson 2, Task 1
Listen and write
Listen to Richard's lecture on hazardous materials at ZemTeQ. Note down your answers to the three questions.

Good afternoon. Let's start. Today we will discuss dangerous substances. They are normally categorized by the harm they cause to people. Normally, substances are put in one or more of the following types.

First, explosive or flammable substances, like organic solvents or petroleum. These can explode or catch fire very easily, resulting in serious burns and injury.

Secondly, harmful substances – which are the most common type – such as chemical cleansers. If they are swallowed, inhaled or they penetrate the skin, they may have a limited health risk.

Irritants can result in allergic reactions like skin or lung swelling after contact. Examples can include some glues, bleaches or solvents like acetone.

Corrosive substances attack by burning people or materials. Examples include strong acids and alkalis like sulphuric acid or caustic soda.

Substances that are toxic stop parts of the body working properly, such as the heart, liver or kidneys. These are called 'poisonous' and include lead, mercury, pesticides and carbon monoxide.

Carcinogens are substances that cause cancer and can include asbestos, hardwood dust and creosote.

Other types of hazardous substances include agents of anoxia, narcotics and oxidizing agents, which you can find out about in the library or from your line manager. Thanks, I think we will break for a coffee at this point.

▶ **Track 8**
Unit 10, Lesson 2, Task 2
Listen and complete
Listen to the lecture again and complete the table with the missing information.
[repeat of Track 7]

▶ Track 9

Unit 10, Lesson 7, Task 1

Listen and write

Listen to the conversation and write the missing words and phrases.

J Richard, hello. I'm in a bit of a pickle.

R Morning, Jimmy. What's the problem?

J Well, I've locked my keys in the car with my books and the important report my boss wants to see today. What an idiot I am! What should I do?

R Calm down. Why not call home for a spare key?

J Nobody's home. And my mobile's in the car.

R OK. You should explain to your boss and tell him you will bring it tomorrow.

J No way. He will kill me. He's going to fire me for this.

R No he won't. Look, I have the solution. I have a hammer in my car. I will smash the window and you can get it repaired in ZemTeQ's vehicle repair centre later.

J That's it. I suppose there isn't another way. Which car park are you in?

▶ Track 10

Unit 11, Lesson 1, Task 1

Listen and write

You are going to listen to Richard's lecture on the dangers of electricity and complete the table. Listen a second time if necessary.

Welcome. You can't see it, you can't smell it and if you feel it, well maybe it's game over. It's a killer. What is it …? Yep, electricity.

The normal dangers with electricity are:

Firstly, shock, which involves electricity flowing through the body – causing spasms in muscles. This can lead to serious injury.

Next, burns, when equipment is overloaded or short-circuits and contact is made. Burns can be on skin and inside the body – this can cause death.

Arc eyes condition is from looking at electrical arc or welding flashes, leading to serious eye problems.

More than 25% of fires in ZemTeQ are due to lack of care, poor maintenance and malfunction of electrical equipment. Even overloaded plugs can create electrical fires.

Lastly, static, which can cause shock or produce sparks and act on a source of ignition with flammable liquids, dusts or powders present.

There are some ways you can prevent injury with electricity. So, think and remember.

Think about supply: Do you know about earth connections? What's an RCD?

Think equipment: What's double insulation?

Think plugs: Is it suitable? Is the cable sheath clamped? What is a fuse?

Think cable: Is it flexible? What capacity does it have? Is it in good condition? Did you inspect it?

Think appliance: Is it in good condition? Is it wired properly? How do you know?

Finally, think inspection: Who inspected the equipment? Does it have an inspection date tag?

▶ Track 11

Unit 11, Lesson 1, Task 2

Listen for key words

Richard's lecture contains many questions about electrical safety. Listen to it again and complete the sentences.

[repeat of Track 10]

▶ Track 12

Unit 11, Lesson 1, Task 3

Listen and categorize

Listen to the lecture one more time and decide what each question is asking about. Mark each question S for supply, E for equipment, P for plugs, C for cables, A for appliances or I for inspection.

[repeat of Track 10]

▶ Track 13

Unit 11, Lesson 7, Task 1

Listen and write

Listen to the conversation and write the missing words and phrases.

J Morning, Richard.

R Hello, Jimmy. What happened to your leg?

J I had an accident in my car on Monday. I hit a tree, which led to this, a broken leg and me on crutches for six weeks.

R Ouch. That must have hurt. What caused the accident?

J Mainly, it was due to my cat.

R You're pulling my leg.

J No, seriously, my cat made noises all night, so I didn't sleep. That meant I overslept and resulted in me rushing in the morning …

R Yes, go on.

J Well, I took a short cut to work, when suddenly an animal jumped into the road, and led to me swerving and bang … here I am. Want to buy a cat?

R Can't stand cats, Jimmy. Never mind. Let me take your book while you go over what we did last week. Your turn to buy the coffee … I think.

▶ **Track 14**

Unit 12, Lesson 4, Task 1

Listen and decide

Listen to the first part of the lecture and mark these statements true (T) or false (F).

Part 1

Hello guys, it's me again. We are here today to think about basic first aid to help people with serious injuries. Do you know where the first-aid box is? Do you know who the first aider is in your section? What do you do in an emergency situation? The important thing to say is you must do some first-aid training. What I will tell you will not equip you to deal with the situation, I will just explain a little about what you need to think about. So go and get that training. If you find someone in an emergency situation, the four priorities are:

1 check the situation – do not put yourself in danger

2 make the area safe

3 look after unconscious people first

4 send for help

Then attend the injured person – check for a response. Gently shake the shoulder and ask loudly 'Are you all right?' If there is no response:

1 shout for help

2 open the airway

3 check for normal breathing

4 take the correct action

▶ **Track 15**

Unit 12, Lesson 4, Task 2

Listen and write

Listen again and write the missing words and phrases.

[repeat of Track 14]

▶ **Track 16**

Unit 12, Lesson 4, Task 4

Listen and choose

Listen to the next part of the lecture. Tick the statement that is true.

Part 2

Think of it as ABC.

A is for airway. Open the airway.

a Put your hand on his forehead.

b Tilt his head back gently.

c Lift chin with two fingers.

B is for breathing. You know … look, listen and feel for normal breath. If breathing is OK, put in recovery position. Plus, get help. If not breathing normally, a trained CPR person is needed.

C is for CPR. Cardiopulmonary resuscitation. Cardio refers to heart, pulmonary to lungs and breathing and resuscitation to starting again. You want them to start breathing and their heart to start beating again.

So, you press on their chest and help them to start breathing. I won't say more, you must get training to do CPR properly. But do it! You could save somebody's life – at work, in the street, even at home.

▶ **Track 17**

Unit 12, Lesson 4, Task 5

Listen and write

Listen again and write the missing words and phrases.

[repeat of Track 16]

▶ **Track 18**

Unit 12, Lesson 7, Task 1

Listen and write

Listen to the conversation and write the missing words and phrases.

J Hello, Richard. How are things?

R Fine, just fine. Well, there is one small thing. How do I get a parking permit?

J Phew … Do you have any good friends in Admin?

R No, I don't.

J Bad luck. Well, the first thing is to go up to Level 3 and get a form. Fill it in, then go to services and get a signature.

R Is that it?

J No, no. Next, go back to Level 3 and get a request form. Again, fill it in and then, finally, you get your line manager to sign it and send it back to Level 3.

R Wow … maybe it is easier to get the bus or a lift from someone.

J Oh, it's not so bad. It will take a couple of days, tops. That's nothing. My friend just got a new ID badge. It took nine weeks! Anyway, good luck.

R Thanks, Jimmy. I owe you. By the way, you don't drive past my house on your way, do you?

▶ **Track 19**
Unit 13, Lesson 2, Task 2
Listen and answer
Listen to Richard's lecture and answer these questions.

Hello, I hope you are all well and have eaten a good breakfast. Today we will think about accident or incident report forms. These record information after an incident, be that an accident, near miss or dangerous occurrence. From these reports, we hope to learn from our mistakes and prevent incidents in the future. Each company's report forms are a little different, sometimes different departments have different forms. Anyway, this is ZemTeQ's form.

The first part has personal details of both the injured person and the report's author, stuff like name and job ID, for example. The top right-hand section gives some information about the date and time of the accident and where it happened. Some reports like to put the injury detail and estimated absence from work.

The second section deals with a short account of the accident details, i.e., what happened. It answers the important questions like what, when, where, who and how. Below this section, on the left-hand side, the report form asks for immediate causes. These may be substandard actions like horseplay, incorrect handling or

working without a permit. Or, they may be substandard conditions that include damaged PPE, poor housekeeping, etc., as the cause. To the right of this is usually a tick box list of the kind of accident that happened. There are 15 types, for example: struck by moving vehicle, exposure to hazardous substances, and so on.

The final few sections need the details of witnesses and signatures. Although, before that, the author is asked to write their conclusions, which is about what we can do to prevent similar future incidents. And that, everyone, is the generalized accident or incident form. But I'm sure the one you will use will be a little different. Everything changes in ZemTeQ week by week.

▶ **Track 20**
Unit 13, Lesson 2, Task 3
Listen and write
Listen again and fill in the missing terms (A–L) on the report.
[repeat of Track 19]

▶ **Track 21**
Unit 13, Lesson 7, Task 1
Listen and write
Listen to the conversation and write the missing words and phrases.

J Hello, Richard. You look worried. What's the matter?

R Oh, hello, Jimmy. Yes, I am. I've lost my bag. It has some large cheques in it and my wallet.

J OK, take it easy. What does it look like?

R Well, it's a bag … er … a briefcase, with a handle and my name on it.

J Right. What size is it?

R Well … it's quite large. About 80 by 50.

J And what colour is it?

R It's black, with a gold security lock. And a black handle.

J How old is it?

R Brand new. I bought it last week.

J And what's it made of?

R It's made of very expensive leather.

J OK, you need to go to lost property and talk to Sammy. He will help you. I'll look around here.

Transcripts

R Cheers, Jimmy. Er ... what does Sammy look like?

J Well, he's very tall and ...

▶ ## Track 22
Unit 14, Lesson 1, Task 3
Listen and write

Listen to Richard talk about eight of the subjects from Task 2. Write them in order.

Morning, today we're going to look back at some of the main health hazards in the workplace. But there will be one or two new ones, too.

We looked at equipment hazards including friction, cutting, shearing, stabbing, impact and crushing for larger machines and also hazards with hand tools. What do you remember about guards?

We also talked about transport safety with vehicles and pedestrians. Remember, this includes mechanical handling as well. What are the main hazards for pedestrians?

We looked at different areas of access, for example: slips, trips and falls, falling or moving objects, working at height, but could also include excavations and confined spaces. What are the key problems with ladders? Can you remember? It could save your life. Your friend's life.

Do you remember handling, both mechanical and manual? What were the rules for lifting? We looked at electrical safety, with shock, burns and fire, for example. How do you treat shock? What do you do if you find someone after an electric shock?

For chemical safety, there were irritants, corrosives and others. What were they? What signs do you remember?

For fire safety, we thought about flammable materials and fire types. Do you remember the types of fire? What extinguishers do you use for each fire type? Were you listening? What do you know about fire procedures? We haven't looked at radiation ... yet, or biological hazards in detail, and these are part of the environmental hazards we will look at soon, including noise, vibration and ergonomics. Do you know what these environmental hazards are? What's the noise limit at work? What is ergonomics?

Well, I hope you know the answers to most of these questions, or I can look for a new job. Thank you.

▶ ## Track 23
Unit 14, Lesson 1, Task 4
Listen and match

Look at the list of words for a minute. Listen to the lecture introduction again and tick the words you hear. Then match each word to a subject from Task 3.

[repeat of Track 22]

▶ ## Track 24
Unit 14, Lesson 7, Task 1
Listen and write

Listen to the conversation and write the missing words and phrases.

J Hi. Where are you off to?

R What? Oh, hello, Jimmy. Sorry, I've got an ear infection so I'm completely deaf today. Can you repeat that, please?

J I said ... where are you going?

R Growing? Sorry, can you speak up a little please?

J Doesn't matter. Do you fancy a cuppa? I'm going to the canteen.

R Supper? A bit early, but I could do with a bite. Thanks.

J Excuse me, Richard. Hello? Oh, hi, Paul. Yes, yes, OK, you want to meet for lunch, where? OK, can you spell that? O-C-E-A-N-I-A restaurant, yes, yeah, I'll find it. At 12? OK. See you later.

R Was that the boss?

J No, my buddy. He wants to take me to a new restaurant for lunch. Want to come?

R Punch? Sorry, can you speak more slowly?

J Lunch, Richard, lunch. My shout.